NEW TESTAMENT
EVERYDAY BIBLE STUDY SERIES

JAMES AND
GALATIANS

SCOT MCKNIGHT

QUESTIONS WRITTEN BY

BECKY CASTLE MILLER

HarperChristian
Resources

New Testament Everyday Bible Study Series: James and Galatians
© 2022 by Scot McKnight

Requests for information should be addressed to:
HarperChristian Resources, 3900 Sparks Dr. SE, Grand Rapids, Michigan
49546

ISBN 978-0-310-12955-4 (softcover)
ISBN 978-0-310-12956-1 (ebook)

HarperChristian Resources titles may be purchased in bulk for church,
business, fundraising, or ministry use. For information, please e-mail
ResourceSpecialist@ChurchSource.com.

First Printing December 2021 / Printed in the United States of America

CONTENTS

GALATIANS

For John and Karen ("Baby Luv")
Phelps and Team Phelps

GENERAL INTRODUCTION

Christians make a claim for the Bible not made of any other book. Or, because the Bible is a library shelf of many authors, it's a claim we make of no other shelf of books. We claim that God worked in each of the authors as they were writing so that what was scratched on papyrus expressed what God wanted communicated to the people of God. Which makes the New Testament a book unlike any other book. Which is why Christians are reading the New Testament almost two thousand years later with great delight. These books have the power to instruct us and to rebuke us and to correct us and to train us to walk with God every day. We read these books because God speaks to us in them.

Developing a routine of reading the Bible with an open heart, a receptive mind, and a flexible will is the why of the *New Testament Everyday Bible Studies*. But not every day will be the same. Some days we pause and take it in and other days we stop and repent and lament and open ourselves to God's restoring graces. No one word suffices for what the Bible does to us. In fact, the Bible's view of the Bible can be found by reading Psalm 119, the longest chapter in the Bible with 176 verses! It is a meditation on eight terms for what the Bible is and what the Bible does to those who listen and read it. Its laws (*torah*) instruct us, its laws (*mishpat*) order us, its statutes direct us, its precepts inform us, its decrees guide us, its commands compel us, its words speak to us, and its promises comfort us. No wonder that the author can sum all eight up as the "way" (119:3, 37). Each of those terms still speaks to what happens when we open our minds to the Word of God.

Every day with the Bible, then, is new because our timeless and timely God communes with us in our daily lives in our world and in our time. Just as God spoke to Jesus in Galilee and Paul in Ephesus and John on Patmos. These various contexts help us hear God in our context so the *New Testament Everyday Bible Studies* will often delve into contexts.

Most of us now have a Bible on our devices. We may well have several translations available to us everywhere we go every day. To hear those words, we are summoned by God to open the Bible, to attune our hearts to God, and to listen to what God says. My prayer is that these Bible study guides will help each of us become daily Bible readers attentive to the mind of God.

JAMES

INTRODUCTION: READING THE LETTER OF JAMES

James, brother of Jesus, was surrounded by four brothers—Jesus, Joseph, Simon, and Judas—and more than one sister, whose names are not known. And, of course, he had a famous mother, Mary. It is likely that Joseph, husband of Mary, was taken in death, leaving Mary to nurture these kids into the faith. That James has a heart for widows and orphans takes this brief letter into their living room (James 1:27). We don't know the date, but James the brother of Jesus was the most influential leader of the church of Jerusalem and was killed in 62 AD. The letter seems to be aware at least of some misunderstandings of Paul's teachings, so dating it in the late 40s but probably in the 50s is about as close as we can get.

I offer a few suggestions on how to read this letter:

First, don't let it slip from your memory that James was Jewish, and he wrote this letter to fellow Jewish believers who had been exiled from the land of their birth. He calls them the "twelve tribes scattered" in 1:1.

Second, think carefully about what words mean by

reading the major words in light of the whole letter. It's too easy for us to slip from "trials" to our computer's glitches. I offer observations about terms like "trial" and "wealth" and "poverty" because when we read the whole letter in light of those terms we see so much more.

Third, this letter wonderfully exhibits early Christian wisdom about a variety of topics such as hot-headed speech patterns and teachers and verbal abusers and trials and reckless merchants and exploiting bosses and how early Christians kowtowed to the rich in spite of how those very rich people were treating them. All of this is bathed in James' wisdom.

Fourth, as you read the letter, jot in the margins of the book or in your Bible cross references to the teachings of Jesus. You will be surprised how often James sounds like his older brother, but I wait until James 5:12 to clarify what's going on.

Finally, James fearlessly addresses our speech patterns so often that we have to duck to miss his points. What may be most relevant about this book is wisdom for how to conduct ourselves on social media.

FOR FURTHER READING

Richard Bauckham, *James* (London: Routledge, 1999).

P. J. Hartin, *James* (Sacra Pagina 14; Collegeville, MN: Liturgical Press, 2003).

Scot McKnight, *The Letter of James*, New International

Commentary on the New Testament (Grand
Rapids: Wm. B. Eerdmans, 2011).

David Nystrom, *James*, NIV Application Commentary
(Grand Rapids: Zondervan, 1997).

Elsa Tamez, *The Scandalous Message of James* (New
York: Crossroads, 2002).

A WISE FAITH

James 1:1–11

[1] *James, a servant of God and of the Lord Jesus Christ,*
   To the twelve tribes scattered among the nations:
   Greetings.

   [2] *Consider it pure joy, my brothers and sisters, whenever you face trials of many kinds, [3] because you know that the testing of your faith produces perseverance. [4] Let perseverance finish its work so that you may be mature and complete, not lacking anything.*

   [5] *If any of you lacks wisdom, you should ask God, who gives generously to all without finding fault, and it will be given to you. [6] But when you ask, you must believe and not doubt, because the one who doubts is like a wave of the sea, blown and tossed by the wind. [7] That person should not expect to receive anything from the Lord. [8] Such a person is double-minded and unstable in all they do.*

   [9] *Believers in humble circumstances ought to take pride in their high position. [10] But the rich should take pride in their humiliation—since they will pass away like a wild flower. [11] For the sun rises with scorching heat and withers the plant; its blossom falls and its beauty is destroyed. In*

*the same way, the rich will fade away even while they go
about their business.*

James writes this letter to Christians who are a long way
from home (outside the land of Israel). He calls them
siblings, or in the NIV, "brothers and sisters." This is the
most popular term in the New Testament for those who
are in the church of Jesus Christ. Jesus is the Son of God,
and when we are adopted in Christ, we become Jesus' own
family members. As such, we become brothers and sisters.
James, though he could claim authority and power over
others, identifies himself with all those who have chosen
to follow Jesus. He is a brother to all the sisters and brothers. This letter is for siblings in Christ. James addresses his
letter to Jewish siblings, but it reaches out to all siblings,
Jew or gentile.

These siblings are not home. One reason they are not at
home where the language, food, and customs make them
comfortable is what he calls "trials of many kinds" (1:2).
Perhaps these trials drove them from the homeland into a
foreign country, often called *diaspora*. The excitement of
a foreign country for the tourist is exile for the one driven
from home involuntarily. I've visited Israel, Turkey, and
Greece imagining palpable experiences of Jesus and the
apostles. What may be for us an adventure was for them
homelessness. If one reads this letter as an exiled person,
one hears something different than how we read it in the
comfort of a cozy chair with a cup of coffee. James calls
their situation "trials" because where they were has to do
with those trials.

What trials are in mind? They are something happening

to the Christians by someone or something else. In this letter such experiences pile up for the attentive reader: economic oppression, favoritism of the wealthy against the poor (Christians), publicly slandering Jesus, shaming one another, and the rich exploiting the poor. Look in your Bible at these verses: James 1:9, 27; 2:1–9; and 5:1–6. The trials or tests have occurred because they are Christians.

They had memories and plenty of knowledge about their trials, but James wanted them to have more than knowledge. He wanted them and us to have wisdom. *Wisdom grabs information, sorts it out into knowledge, and then discerns the ways of God.* In our passage, James reveals such wisdom. Tests press us deeper into our faith. Think of Dietrich Bonhoeffer, the German martyr under Hitler's National Socialism. His book *Discipleship* has that famous line, "When Christ calls a man, he bids him come and die."[1] That book is famous too for what he said about "cheap grace." We know these things, but Bonhoeffer pierced through knowledge into wisdom. His ideas were formulated, turned into lectures, and then into a book in his own kind of exile, an underground seminary that had to change locations because Hitler's agents were on his case. The trial of the churches to conform to Hitler's will was resisted by Bonhoeffer and produced the wisdom of a book that has challenged us for nine decades. The category of "cheap grace" and the call to follow Jesus, no matter what, was wisdom's deepest challenge for the German churches and has become wisdom for us.

---

1. The official translation is not so poetic. It reads, "Whenever Christ calls us, his call leads us to death." See *Discipleship* (DBW 4; trans. B. Green, R. Krauss; Minneapolis: Fortress, 2001), 87.

What wisdom can we discern from tests and trials and pressures? Only a wise and imaginative faith can "consider it pure joy" in the middle of a storm (1:2). James' kind of faith-shaped imagination prompts us to find wisdom in our tests.

First, tests of our faith promote our growth. James will soon be quick to push back against anyone who slanders God by saying God is a tempter, and we need to let this soak in: the tests we experience are not God's doing but opportunities for us to become mature in our faith. James, like other early followers of Jesus (notice how Romans 5:2–5 and 1 Peter 1:6–7 sound a bit like our passage), grew in wisdom through trials. In his wisdom, James has learned that tests do things. The word he uses ("produces") suggests, promotes, creates, and works itself into something. A tested faith works into *perseverance* (or endurance and resilience). And perseverance transforms us into "mature and complete" siblings, and exiles will hear a core value when James finishes verse four with "not lacking anything" (1:3–4).

The word "maturity," sometimes translated with the word "perfection," matters to James and he uses it several times (1:4, 17, 25; 2:22; 3:2). It does not mean sinlessness (3:2) or perfection as we often use the term. Rather, it evokes the person who reaches the goal, who attains the vision, or who completes the journey. It describes mature moral development in one's relationship to God, to self, and to others. Some people seem to arrive early while most of us need decades. The wise move toward maturity.

Second, tests of our faith require wisdom. We learn wisdom by looking back. In the moments of being tested, we may be totally confused and battling doubts, and that is why James turns from the uplifting idea that tests promote growth to the suggestion that we may well need to turn to God for wisdom. The question for the exiles is the same question we ask today: "What's going on, God?" or, "Why, God?" Those questions are why we turn to God, revealing that wisdom is more than information and knowledge. It is a gift that comes to us by scanning our lives to see what God has given to us. To receive this gift, we must ask God.

To ask God requires that we start with sound theology: God "gives generously" and God gives to us "without finding fault" (1:5). We don't hear God griping with "What a pain that guy has been!" or "You again?!" or "Will you ever grow up?" James reminds us that our requests begin with the wisdom that God is not only good and generous but that God answers. Jesus taught the very same thing in Matthew 7:7–11.

Wise faith trusts and does not doubt. This is one of those either-or statements that looks only at the ends of a spectrum: most of us trust with some doubt or even doubt with a little bit of trust. James presses the distinction as a way of exhorting the Christians to trust the generosity of God. He's like a father teaching a daughter to dive off the 10–foot diving board the first time into the pool by saying, "Jump, you'll be alright. Go ahead. You'll never know how fun and easy it is until you jump." Most jump and learn and easily forget how difficult the first jump was. (Someone say "Amen!")

Trusting God to be generous, even for those with this mixture of faith and doubt, evokes a Galilean Sea image. Mixing faith and doubt is like being in a boat tossed by the waves. (I get dizzy, sometimes more than that, thinking about it.) James pushes harder by saying the doubting-believer is "double-minded" and "unstable in all they do" (1:8). James grew up daily reciting what we call the *Shema* from Deuteronomy 6, which exhorted him to love God with *all* his heart. To be double-minded splits the heart. The double-minded person experiences trials as chaos even though our good God, who turns chaos into order (Genesis 1), generously offers a clarity that calms the chaotic waters.

Let's tie this into a simple observation: if God is one who gives without reprimanding us, then we are to be persons who ask without doubting God. God, it can be said, is simply good—good in all God does—so we are to be simply trusting—trusting in all we do. Wise persons have learned by trusting God that God is trustworthy, which itself leads them to trust God again and again.

Third, tests of our faith give us social perspective. The exiles knew a rock-solid reality: believers were poor, and the wealthy, who had fancy clothing and traveled to far-off countries, were not believers. Their role models were people like Simeon and Anna (Luke 2:25–38), and they sang Mary's song (the Magnificat, Luke 1:46–55) the way you may be singing Lauren Daigle's *You Say*. However much a stereotype, the connection of believer with poverty and wealthy with unbeliever was accurate around 98 percent of the time (read James 2:1–7 and 5:1–6).

I like this turnabout: it is the poor who are actually wealthy, and the wealthy who are actually poor! We can add a verse to Lauren Daigle's song: *You say I am rich when I am feeling poor.* Yes, the poor experiencing economic downturns and oppression are the ones in the "high position" (1:9), while the rich exploiters are in a state of "humiliation" (1:10). Why? Riches, as James' glorious Lord Jesus taught him, don't last (Matt. 6:19–34). Grabbing an image from his Bible, though we are not sure from which book (Ps. 90:3–6 or 103:15–16 or Isa. 40:6–8?), or perhaps spotting it on the Galilean hillsides, James sketches for all of us the impermanence of riches by comparing it to a "wild flower" (James 1:10–11): the sun's heat withers the plant, the flower falls off, the plant dies. The rich businessmen—notice how James finishes with "go about their business," and now look at 4:13 17 and their riches will fade away like one of these scorched wild flowers.

What lasts? Being loved in God's generous love and care. That's information and knowledge, but wisdom takes it into the heart, turns to God, and trusts God come what may. Even in exile.

QUESTIONS FOR REFLECTION AND APPLICATION

1. James writes an oft-quoted verse in this first chapter: "Consider it pure joy . . . whenever you face trials of many kinds." McKnight helps us understand that James' readers were going through something significant because they were Christians. What trials did he suggest come to mind based on the entire book of James? What might you consider to be "trials of many kinds" for Christians in North America?

2. McKnight writes, "Tests do things." What are three things that tests do according to James, as covered in this section?

3. How would you explain wisdom? McKnight writes, *"Wisdom grabs information, sorts it out into knowledge, and then discerns the ways of God."* What do you think of this explanation of wisdom? (In 3:13–18 McKnight defines wisdom as "living in God's world in God's way.")

4. How might your social media usage (or your personal conversations) change if you were "quick to listen, slow to speak and slow to become angry"?

5. What is a trial or challenge you are facing that you can look at as an opportunity for growth? How does that shift in perspective change your approach?

FOR FURTHER READING

Eberhard Bethge, *Dietrich Bonhoeffer: A Biography* (Minneapolis: Fortress, 2000), 419–586.

Dietrich Bonhoeffer, *Discipleship*, DBW 4; trans. B. Green, R. Krauss (Minneapolis: Fortress, 2001).

Scot McKnight, "Poverty, Riches, and God's Blessings: James in the Context of the Biblical Story," in Eric F. Mason, Darian R. Lockett, *Reading the Epistle of James: A Resource for Students* (Resources for Biblical Study 94; Atlanta: SBL Press, 2019), 161–175.

WISE BASICS

James 1:12–21

[12] *Blessed is the one who perseveres under trial because, having stood the test, that person will receive the crown of life that the Lord has promised to those who love him.*

[13] *When tempted, no one should say, "God is tempting me." For God cannot be tempted by evil, nor does he tempt anyone;* [14] *but each person is tempted when they are dragged away by their own evil desire and enticed.* [15] *Then, after desire has conceived, it gives birth to sin; and sin, when it is full-grown, gives birth to death.*

[16] *Don't be deceived, my dear brothers and sisters.* [17] *Every good and perfect gift is from above, coming down from the Father of the heavenly lights, who does not change like shifting shadows.* [18] *He chose to give us birth through the word of truth, that we might be a kind of firstfruits of all he created.*

[19] *My dear brothers and sisters, take note of this: Everyone should be quick to listen, slow to speak and slow to become angry,* [20] *because human anger does not produce the righteousness that God desires.* [21] *Therefore, get rid of all moral filth and the evil that is so prevalent and humbly accept the word planted in you, which can save you.*

I grew up in a community with some German background and so (seemingly) we alone knew that our high school sports teams' nickname, the "Pretzels," had a cultured history. This did not mean our athletic opponents, and then eventually ESPN, didn't have fun at our expense. It did mean we had the opportunity to take German in junior high. My first teacher, Frau Meinders, was marvelous. We began with the basics: the alphabet, which had some pronunciations of common letters that we had to learn. Then, speaking and reading the types of sentences we learned in Dr. Seuss' *The Cat and the Hat* or readers with sentences like "Watch Spot run," we learned the basics: nouns and verbs. Over and over. Every day. Until they stuck in our heads. Frau Meinders would say, *"Wiederholen Sie!"* (Repeat.) She said it, we said it, she said it, we said it. Ask a question in English, she answered in German. No messing around with her.

Once a student asked what the German term for "bright" was. All five-foot-one of her spread her arms wide, scanning the classroom and its light, and said, *"Es ist hell."* We all snickered, even she got rosy cheeks with the fun of it all, and then we all learned to use the term "hell" (bright) mischievously. We graduated to high school, and our new German teacher, Herr Kurr, was just as good. We were stuck if we hadn't mastered what Frau Meinders taught us. Want me to sing "The Age of Aquarius" *auf Deutsch*? We learned the basics so we could then read serious stuff and speak with some degree of fluency. I spent two summers in Austria evangelizing *auf Deutsch*. I'm grateful for those two teachers teaching me the basics. I am grateful, too, for James giving us three basic lessons for following Jesus in our world.

The first verse (1:12) in this passage summarizes what James wrote in the previous passage and strikes a chord common to the whole Bible: we live before God, there is a judgment, and God's evaluation is right. So, the first basic lesson is to *keep your eye on the prize of all prizes*. The trials and tests of the siblings in exile—especially economic injustices—challenged them to endurance ("perseveres"). We might be tempted to think "stood the test" means something like hanging on or sticking it out, but it favors the sense of "proven genuine" as in 1 Peter 1:6–7. In James, one is proven genuine by loving the Lord ("to those who love him," James 1:12). Here James stimulates his readers by appealing to their life-long habit of reciting the *Shema* ("Hear O Israel . . . love the LORD your God") and by summarizing the whole of life, including enduring tests with faithfulness, as a life of loving God. To love God is a faithful, rugged, and affective commitment to God that leads us to spend time with God, to bring God glory, and to surrender to the gracious transforming powers of God.

Two expressions in this verse announce that the prize of all prizes is God's approval: "blessed" and the granting of a "crown of life." Blessed transcends what we call happiness and has no time for smiley-face translations. The term describes God's approval into the divine presence where we bask in God's company. Those blessed love the Lord in faithfulness—again not in sinless perfection. Obedience as blessing and disobedience as curse shape the covenant God makes with humans (Deut. 27–28; Luke 6:20–26). Jesus' beatitudes in Luke evoke a theme James uses in James 1:9–11: reversal. Those blessed are not celebrities or the famous but those who in this life gain little attention and honor. God sees the heart, and humans don't. These are ones given a prize, the "crown of life," or the crown that is life evermore. The crown is an image drawn from athletic contests, but what matters here is eternal life. God doesn't design a crown to stimulate competition with others but to encourage us to faithful devotion.

The blessing of eternal life has waned among the current generation. All talk of hell and heaven have fallen into the ditch along the path. Someday, James reminds us, we will stand before God so we may need to remind ourselves all over again of this basic lesson.

The second basic lesson is *God is not the problem. We are.* Humans blame God with "God is tempting me" (1:13). No, James says with double emphasis, not only is God untemptable but God never tempts anyone. James plays with a term here: the word behind "trials" in 1:2 and 1:12 and "tempt" in 1:13–14 is the same (*peirasmos* the noun and its verb *peirazō*). One could translate all of them as "tests" or "tempts," but that doesn't quite work because every test carries with it a temptation for a human to fail growth in wisdom. Depending on the context and sense, we translate the term either "test" or "tempt." Here it means tempt. God is good, God is generous (1:5), and all gifts from God are perfectly good from the unchangingly good God (1:16–18). These truths imply that God is never evil and stingy and that God never tempts anyone. Ever. So, James has learned as a basic lesson that, if we are tempted, it is our problem.

Very few texts reflect perception of the self and sin as does the Bible. James gets theoretical here like a good teacher. Read these two verses aloud, and give emphasis to the italicized words as they develop James' "theory" of sin:

But each person is tempted when they are dragged away by *their own evil desire* and enticed. Then, after desire has *conceived*, it *gives birth to sin*; and sin, when it is full-grown, *gives birth to death* (1:14–15).

Here's his theory: desire entices to sin and sin gives birth to death. Death counters the crown of life in 1:12 just as loving God is countered by desire and sin. James' second basic lesson, in other words, then is *take responsibility for your temptations and your sins*. Like Jesus, he knows that "what comes out of a person defiles them" and that "evil thoughts come" and pop up from inside us (Mark 7:20–21). Maybe James (not Jesus) had heard of Paul's teachings: "For I do not do the good I want to do, but the evil I do not want to do—this I keep on doing" (Rom. 7:19). Jesus, Paul, and James drive a fat wedge between temptation and God. And they were all three aware of the Jewish sense that all humans have two *yetzers*, or two desires/wills. We have a good *yetzer* and a bad *yetzer*. Each battles us inside. In fact, one rabbinic text says the righteous are swayed by their good *yetzer*, the wicked by their evil *yetzer*, and the average person by both *yetzers*! (James would call this person double-minded.)

The all-too-human reflex of blaming God deceives us into making an excuse. God does not change; God sends down gifts that are "good and perfect." Instead of blaming God, we need to look to the God who transforms our desires so we can become witnesses—"firstfruits"—of God's grace in this world. How does this transformation occur? James points a long finger at the very "desires" he has in mind: social media! Not really, but if he were alive today, he would say that. Instead, he points at listening problems, speech problems, and anger problems (1:19–20; see also 4:1–12). An evangelist friend of mine told me recently that we need to ask more questions than we answer and listen more than we speak. James amens those wise words because he has learned this problem from long experience with hotheads in the Holy Land. Ever hear of the Zealots, those who were quick to think war was the way to solve problems? Or the Sicarii (a sect of the Zealots), who were quick to pull out daggers from under their belts? Watching people respond to Jesus, and no doubt knowing a multitude of stories about how his critics reacted to Jesus, James had developed the kind of wisdom that settled into this statement: "human anger does not produce the righteousness that God desires" (1:20). Or, human anger, the anger of the hotheads of James 1 and James 4, never leads to what is right. (James is not discussing the kind of anger that is a force for good.)

This is James' third basic lesson: *transformation is an inside-out process*. Basic vocabulary in the way of Jesus is that we have been given a (new) "birth through the word of truth" (1:18) and that we are "humbly [to] accept the word planted" in us (1:21). Maybe James has heard the story about Nicodemus and "new birth" (John 3) and perhaps also Paul's term "regeneration" (Titus 3:5). In these two verses he's on the same page, one line above or below or in the margin, in speaking of God's "word"—does he mean Jesus as the Logos, as the Word of God in John 1:1–14, or the gospel message as logos or the truth of God as logos? (Yes.) This word has been "implanted" or, to coin a new word, it has become "in-natured" into us. Expand what you think of this idea by looking at 1:18 (truth), 1:21 (saving), 1:25 (perfect freedom-creating law), 2:8 (royal law), and 4:5 (Spirit). Get this: James teaches that God's grace can become second nature to us. If our first nature is to desire sin and death, and if our first nature blames God, the new second nature transforms us to desire God's righteousness and to love God and to endure tests with wisdom and to grow into maturity. It starts inside and works itself out.

Three basic lessons: keep your eye on the prize, God is not the problem, and transformation is an inside-out process. Just like learning German from Frau Meinders.

QUESTIONS FOR REFLECTION AND APPLICATION

1. What does "crown of life" mean to you? How does the idea of that prize waiting for you impact your daily life?

2. How does this lesson define loving God? What do you think of that definition, and how would loving God in this way work in your life?

3. What are James' three basic lessons, in your own words?

4. What is a *yetzer*? Think about a time you felt the tension of good and evil *yetzers* inside yourself. How did you resolve the inner conflict?

5. What are some inner-to-outer transformations you have seen God make in your life since you started following Jesus?

FOR FURTHER READING

J. Marcus, "The Evil Inclination in the Epistle of James,"
    CBQ 44 (1982), 606–621.

Babylonian Talmud, Berakoth 61b.

Scot McKnight, *Pastor Paul: Nurturing a Culture
    of Christoformity in the Church* (Grand Rapids:
    Brazos, 2019), 41–48.

Patrick Mitchel, *The Message of Love: The Only Thing
    That Counts* (London: IVP UK, 2019).

WISE DOERS

James 1:22–27

22 Do not merely listen to the word, and so deceive yourselves. Do what it says. 23 Anyone who listens to the word but does not do what it says is like someone who looks at his face in a mirror 24 and, after looking at himself, goes away and immediately forgets what he looks like. 25 But whoever looks intently into the perfect law that gives freedom, and continues in it—not forgetting what they have heard, but doing it—they will be blessed in what they do.

26 Those who consider themselves religious and yet do not keep a tight rein on their tongues deceive themselves, and their religion is worthless. 27 Religion that God our Father accepts as pure and faultless is this: to look after orphans and widows in their distress and to keep oneself from being polluted by the world.

Some passages in the Bible are a little too clear for comfort, and this passage may be one of them for you. I know it is for me. As C. S. Lewis said, forgiveness is a great idea until you are the one who has to do the forgiving, this passage is also a great idea until it taps firmly on your shoulder. James grabs our attention with two firm words: "hearing" and "doing." To hear the word is to hear God's voice speaking to us in Christ, in the Spirit, through the Word. To hear is to learn what God wants from us. Doing the word hears that voice and then lives it.

So James wants us to read our Bibles and listen for God to speak, which is all to the good. He then tells us that we are to be "doers of the word," which is good too, but his next lines can take our breath away: only those who do the word are the God-blessed ones. A few verses later he says much the same, "Religion . . . [that is] pure and faultless" with God is a hearing that does (1:27). James has now more than tapped on the shoulder. He's about to let us in on the greatest mystery of life: how we relate well to God. He's got our attention, and we are perhaps now asking questions. Like: Isn't this a little too close to thinking we earn our way to God? Or, aren't we secure by God's grace and not by what we do? James would answer No and then Yes, and he still taps on our shoulder because he is exhorting us to grow in doing.

During the shelter in place of COVID-19, Kris and I worked on jigsaw puzzles, including what became our favorite, called "I Am Lion." It is a gorgeous head of a male lion with intricate color shifts and no rectangle border—so it was also our most challenging puzzle. The eyes are majestic, and they don't turn away. Lions in zoos tend to look by us or through us, but this puzzle's lion looks at us. So taken were we by our "I Am Lion" puzzle that we have now glued it and attached it to a foam board and have it hanging on a wall. Problem is, the puzzle is on the wall in the room where I do Zoom conferences, and that lion's constant stare does two things at once: it reveals the beauty and the fierceness of a male lion. A kind of comfort and discomfort all at once.

James 1:22–27 is like the lion. It can be comforting to hear the clarity of God's message, and it can be especially comforting to remember that God is at work in us through the Spirit and the "implanted word" (see 1:21). But discomforting because of the specific examples of what it means to be a doer of God's word. James intends our discomfort to motivate us to grow as doers of the word. James calls the word "the perfect law that gives freedom." This shows he thinks the law of Moses is fulfilled in the teachings of Jesus that shape the whole law by the Jesus Creed, the response Jesus gave to a scribe when he asked about the most important commandment in the Bible. Jesus' "creed" was to love God and to love others (Mark 12:28–34). In James 1:12, the ultimate approval is for those who love God; in 1:26–27, divine approval is for those who look after the marginalized; and in 2:8–10, he says the same of those who love their neighbor as themselves. Thus, he is teaching what Jesus taught. The word and law of freedom are clear and have a fierce stare.

We must be reminded both of our need to do what we hear (and read) and of what doing the word means in real life. Verses 26–27 tell us what "doing" is:

1. controlling the tongue,
2. compassion for the marginalized, and
3. avoiding worldliness.

It would be easy to think that these three are all there are. Yet any reader of the Bible knows they are particular instances, and others could be mentioned too. Isaiah, in one of his beautiful poems, focused on "those who walk righteously and speak what is right, who reject gain from extortion and keep their hands from accepting bribes, who stop their ears against plots of murder and shut their eyes against contemplating evil" (33:15). Paul talks about the fruit of the Spirit (Gal. 5:22–23), and Jesus' Sermon on the Mount (Matt. 5–7) gives yet other particulars. All of them add up to a good character transformed by God—in other words, to what James calls "doing the word." Let's look more closely at each of James' expressions.

First, doing the word means wise speech. No one talks about control of the tongue in the Bible more than James, and most of James 3 is devoted to the topic, and in fierce terms. For him, like his older brother Jesus (Matt. 15:10–20), what comes out of the mouth comes from what's inside. How one spoke was always important in Israel, in early Christianity, and it was important as well in the Greco-Roman world (where this letter arrived). What we say comes from the heart and reveals the heart. Lauren Winner's book *The Dangers of Christian Practice* informs us that practices over time that are stained with sin and the flesh lead, not to spiritual formation, but to spiritual *de*formation. The same can be said about the tongue and social media. The habitual, relentless practice of criticizing someone or calling out others deforms us into haters, while the habitual practice of kind words forms us into doers of the word.

Second, doing the word means compassion for the marginalized. The world of James often encountered both orphans and widows. The Old Testament raises their treatment to the top of the ethical list. (See Deut. 16:14; 26:12–13; Jer. 49:11.) God, the Bible tells us, is the "father of orphans and widows" (see Ps. 68:5). In James' world, an "orphan" was not someone who was parent-less but someone who was either father-less or mother-less. The widowing of a mother made her children orphans. Thus, Lamentations 5:3 says, "we have become orphans, [that is,] fatherless, our mothers are like widows" (NRSV). It is an old Christian tradition that Jesus lost his father, Joseph, which would have meant that Jesus and his siblings (Mark 6:3) were orphans and his mother a widow. James knew from experience in Nazareth who had "true worship" because he knew the hands that showed compassion to his brothers, sisters, and mother. Widows today are the most neglected demographic in churches. This awful habit of humans was resisted constantly in the Bible. Caring for the widow is found everywhere (Deut. 10:18; Ps. 146:9; Ezek. 22:7; Luke 7:12; Acts 6:1; 1 Tim. 5:3–5). To limit the marginalized to these two would miss the point, so we need to think as well of the homeless, the incarcerated, the ethnic minorities, women, children, widowers, immigrants, abuse survivors, people with mental illnesses, the unemployed, the aged, and we could go on.

Third, doing the word means walking away from worldliness. We don't use the term "worldly" much anymore, but that's a mistake. Here's why: the world in the Bible is alive, an agent of our destruction, and Jesus, Paul, John, and here James know the difference between what God wants and the ways of the world. In chapter four, James gives us a choice of being a friend of God or a friend of the world (4:4).

He's not asking Christians to withdraw from the world but to be uncontaminated and unstained and unblamed by the world. Worldliness crystallizes in power, indulgence, and selfishness. Too many of us are so shaped by and into the world that we don't recognize the Lion of Judah is staring at us, and he is tapping on our shoulders, too.

QUESTIONS FOR REFLECTION AND APPLICATION

1. Why do you think James and Jesus both focus on the connection between our hearts and our words? Why does wise speech matter for Christians?

2. How would you define "worldliness" in practical terms for today?

3. Look up one of the Old Testament Scriptures mentioned in this lesson. What context and insight do they add to your understanding of James?

4. Which of James' categories of "doing the word" do you find most challenging in your life, and why? Controlling the tongue, compassion for the marginalized, or avoiding worldliness?

5. Think of someone you know who fits one of the marginalized people groups included here. What will you do this week to "do the word" for them?

FOR FURTHER READING

Miriam Neff, *From One Widow to Another: Conversations for the New You* (Chicago: Moody Press, 2009).

Kevin Vanhoozer, *Hearers and Doers* (Bellingham, WA: Lexham Press, 2019).

Lauren Winner, *The Dangers of Christian Practice* (New Haven, CT: Yale University Press, 2018).

WISE DISCERNMENTS

James 2:1–13

²:¹ *My brothers and sisters, believers in our glorious Lord Jesus Christ must not show favoritism.* ² *Suppose a man comes into your meeting wearing a gold ring and fine clothes, and a poor man in filthy old clothes also comes in.* ³ *If you show special attention to the man wearing fine clothes and say, "Here's a good seat for you," but say to the poor man, "You stand there" or "Sit on the floor by my feet,"* ⁴ *have you not discriminated among yourselves and become judges with evil thoughts?*

⁵ *Listen, my dear brothers and sisters: Has not God chosen those who are poor in the eyes of the world to be rich in faith and to inherit the kingdom he promised those who love him?* ⁶ *But you have dishonored the poor. Is it not the rich who are exploiting you? Are they not the ones who are dragging you into court?* ⁷ *Are they not the ones who are blaspheming the noble name of him to whom you belong?*

⁸ *If you really keep the royal law found in Scripture, "Love your neighbor as yourself," you are doing right.* ⁹ *But if you show favoritism, you sin and are convicted by the law as lawbreakers.* ¹⁰ *For whoever keeps the whole law*

and yet stumbles at just one point is guilty of breaking all of it. [11] For he who said, "You shall not commit adultery," also said, "You shall not murder." If you do not commit adultery but do commit murder, you have become a lawbreaker.

[12] Speak and act as those who are going to be judged by the law that gives freedom, [13] because judgment without mercy will be shown to anyone who has not been merciful. Mercy triumphs over judgment.

Kowtowing to the wealthy, to the privileged, to the powerful, and to those in the know happens in every society every day, and in many churches every weekend, and in most churches too often. Events, incidents, and accidents like this unmask social assumptions. Most of us are so intertwined in our social realities that we do not discern the inconsistencies of these incidents with our faith. James is here to help us because we need someone to walk into our assemblies and say, "Hey, friends, something's not right!" We need to listen so we can do.

James sketches a scene. A wealthy man enters "your meeting." The Greek term for "your meeting" is *synagōgē*, which can have three senses: a synagogue building, an assembly of people, or a gathering of messianic Jews who call their meetings what they had called them before they turned to the "Lord Jesus Christ." Since he later uses the word "church" (5:14) and since he uses "your" with meeting and "among yourselves" in our passage, it is reasonable that James thinks of this as an assembly of messianic Jews in a designated space. He focuses on clothing. What one chooses to wear expresses a person's self-perception. (We have too much trendy today, too much fashion show, too much "preachers-n-sneakers.") The rich man dresses the part, and James frames a word and calls him a "gold-fingered" guy. He is given a special seat—perhaps in the front row, at least somewhere comfortable and conspicuous. Entering alongside, no doubt behind, the wealthy man is a poor man dressed in clothing expressing poverty. Instead of being ushered to a seat he is asked to stand somewhere or to sit on the floor. In our terms, the first man's a celebrity. Celebrities are well-known persons who are *celebrated* as special by others. Think of it in reverse. When we celebrate a person for their fame (instead of their faith) we are treating them as celebrities. Only one person deserves celebration in a church, and that's where James started to describe the scene: "the glorious Lord Jesus Christ."

A pragmatic person sees this all go down and says, "That's how life works," or maybe, "We might get some donations out of this guy." A wise person like James observes this happening and says, "This is not right." Pragmatic people lack discernment. Pragmatic people see the surface; wise people see through the surface and discern the moral realities at work under that surface.

What do wise persons discern?

The wise person *identifies the problem with clarity*. No one in the New Testament talks more about the speech patterns than James, but no one else is as pointed as he is in naming some sins. He names this incident "favoritism," and this translates a word that suggests lifting up a person's face to see who it is and to see if they are worthy. A couple questions can illustrate the point. When you buy an article of clothing, do you look at the brand name? And, in doing so, are you thinking of impressing others? Or of quality? (Price, my wife often tells me, is not a good indicator.) When you buy a bottle of wine, do you assume the price indicates whether the wine is good or not? Is your palate actually fine enough even to know the difference? Or are you thinking a cheap wine is below your dignity?

Transfer these common instances of favoritism to how you (mis)treat others—African Americans, Latin Americans, Asian Americans—and that's what "favoritism" means. It means "they" versus "us." It's prejudice, it's bias, it's racism, it's sexism, it's political partisanship, it's snobbery, it's arrogance, and it's wrong. Let us not forget, too, that habits of prejudice become systemic, and systemic prejudice must not only be named but admitted, unraveled, tossed away, and new habits and threads must be woven into a new system of goodness. Most importantly, prejudices both in practice and system are out of line with Jesus who was himself a poor man in poor clothing. Beth Moore speaks to all of us in our muteness: "To sit back and say nothing is to cast a vote of approval."

One of the wisest moves to get people to discern what's under the hood is to *ask good questions.* Our tone in reading James' series of questions in 2:4–7 matters. One can read these in anger, or as a rough interrogation, or as questions probing ordinary folks. (You might try asking James' questions aloud on your own from each angle and then ask which one best suits the passage.) It seems to me he's irritated, and his wisdom turns a tad prophetic. Have you "discriminated" and "become judges with evil thoughts?" (Yes.) A little softer: Has God chosen the poor? (Yes.) Somewhere between the two previous questions: Are the rich exploiting you? (Yes.) A little stronger voice now: Are they hauling you into courts? (Yes.) Are they the ones slandering Jesus' name? (Yes.) Tone aside, the answers matter and the rhetoric does its work: the believers become aware that their actions are prejudice. Celebrity-ism has no part in the church. Kowtowing to the rich is wrong. These questions led the believers to perceive the utter inconsistency between their own oppressed-at-the-hands-of-the-privileged-and-powerful situation and their favor-the-celebrity in their assembly. They knew their own realities: most were poor, the wealthy exploited them, the wealthy took them to court, and the wealthy slandered their own Lord. All by way of questions.

Good questions, when compared to straightforward statements, empower people to answer for themselves, and they permit inner probings. I have learned, too, that good questions often lead to answers I never imagined and open up into unexpected, growing conversations. Sometimes questions lead to responses that show that the question was not a good one but another one is better. Good questions leading to better questions promote wisdom.

Prejudice and love don't hold hands, so wisdom takes us to the *basic of all basics*. Jews began the day and ended the day by reciting the *Shema* ("Hear O Israel . . . Love the LORD your God with all your heart and with all your soul and with all your strength" Deuteronomy 6:4–5). Along came a theological expert asking Jesus which of the commands (*mitzvot*) was the greatest, and Jesus (in effect) encouraged the man to take a seat at his feet and listen up. Here's what he told him: "Love God," which repeats the *Shema*, and "Love your neighbor the way you love yourself," which comes from Leviticus 19. Jesus said that reducing the commands to one is a mistake because there are two: love God, love others. These two commands in the law of Moses become the moral foundation for discipleship to Jesus. Do you love God? Do you love others? Not one without the other, as 1 John says over and over. John wasn't the only one who got into love as the heart of it all. So did Paul, Peter and, James. In 1:12, James mentioned loving God, and now he mentions the other half of Jesus' teaching, which I call the Jesus Creed. Like his older brother, he cites Leviticus 19.

Get this: to love another person as yourself means a rugged, affective commitment to be with that person, to be for that person, and to grow together to be like Christ. Great idea until the person you are called to love happens to be someone you don't like! Or from the other political party. Or doesn't appreciate your privilege and has told you so. To love like Jesus takes our all.

James uses the Jesus Creed to probe the believers even more. If you love your neighbor as yourself, excellent! *Tov!* Beautiful! But, if you show prejudice against the poor and favor to the celebrity—and here James uses the law as he has learned it—"you sin and are convicted by the law as lawbreakers" (2:9). He probes deeper now. If you break one law you are a lawbreaker and that means you are as good as guilty of breaking all 613 of them! The one law James cares about here is the law Jesus made foundational: loving your neighbor as yourself. You can't love your neighbor *and* degrade the status of a person because he's poor or upgrade the status of a person because he's rich and wears $1,500 sneakers on the church platform, can you? So James in his wisdom takes us back to the basic of all basics: love God, love others.

Once again we need to think of the *basics*: we will stand before God to be "judged by the law that gives freedom" (2:12). In James 1:25, James spoke of the "perfect law that gives freedom" and in 2:12 he only drops out "perfect." Because of Jesus, James knows the law (of Moses) as liberating. The law is the measure, but the law as understood by Jesus is loving God and loving others. Which is liberating in that it sets a person free to focus on persons. But a sigh of relief fails the test here. I can hear someone say, "love is better than law," but I answer back, "divine judgment of how well we loved God and loved others is no (as the Germans say it) *Spaziergang*, no lazy walk in the park." In fact, for Jesus, law is the surface, and love is under the surface, and he wants us to dive deep into the depths of love.

James now faces his prejudice-practicing congregation and says, "What you did was wrong. You practiced judgment of fellow believers. Now turn from prejudice to mercy." Mercy here means treating the poor man right and the rich man right, and right means as a sibling. Not as a celebrity, and not as a deplorable. No upgrades, and no downgrades.

You and I are brothers and sisters. Sit next to me.

Just as our glorious Lord Jesus Christ sat with the disciples.

QUESTIONS FOR REFLECTION AND APPLICATION

1. What does James have to say about treating some Christians as celebrities? How could this be applied to changing the current celebrity culture in American Christianity today?

2. What do multiple biblical authors offer as the antidote to prejudice in the church?

3. Try the reading-out-loud exercise in the lesson with James' questions. Which tone do you think best fits what he is communicating?

4. How has favoritism in the church either harmed you or benefitted you?

5. Reflect on any favoritism or celebrity-ism you might hold in your heart. What will you do to shift your perspective toward equality and sibling relationships?

FOR FURTHER READING

Luke Timothy Johnson, *Brother of Jesus, Friend of God: Studies in the Letter of James* (Grand Rapids: Wm. B. Eerdmans, 2004).

Ben Kirby, *PreachersNSneakers: Authenticity in an Age of For-Profit Faith and (Wannabe) Celebrities* (Nashville: Thomas Nelson, 2021).

Beth Moore, with Melissa Moore, *James: Mercy Triumphs* (Nashville: LifeWay, 2011), citing p. 88.

WISE WORKS

James 2:14 26[1]

[14] *What good is it, my brothers and sisters, if someone claims to have faith but has no [works]? Can such faith save them?* [15] *Suppose a brother or a sister is without clothes and daily food.* [16] *If one of you says to them, "Go in peace; keep warm and well fed," but does nothing about their physical needs, what good is it?* [17] *In the same way, faith by itself, if it is not accompanied by [works], is dead.*

[18] *But someone will say, "You have faith; I have [works]."*

Show me your faith without [works], and I will show you my faith by my [works]. [19] *You believe that there is one God. Good! Even the demons believe that—and shudder.*

[20] *You foolish person, do you want evidence that faith*

---

1. The NIV's translators have unfortunately chosen to translate the term works (*erga*) with words like "deeds" and "action." They have also chosen to translate with "considered righteous" rather than "justified." I have edited the translation. Many are uncomfortable with the word "works" because it evokes "works righteousness." The solution is not to shift the word to "deeds," which doesn't solve that problem, but to get the relationship of faith and works and justification right.

without [works] is useless? [21] Was not our father Abraham [justified by works] when he offered his son Isaac on the altar? [22] You see that his faith and his [works] were working together, and his faith was made complete by [works]. [23] And the scripture was fulfilled that says, "Abraham believed God, and it was credited to him as righteousness," and he was called God's friend. [24] You see that a person is [justified by works] and not by faith alone.

[25] In the same way, was not even Rahab the prostitute [justified by works] when she gave lodging to the spies and sent them off in a different direction? [26] As the body without the spirit is dead, so faith without [works] is dead.

Some things are inseparable: grass and green, flower and fragrance, trees and leaves, trains and tracks, home and family pictures, sports and cheering (and booing), oceans and sun, churches and singing, pastors and preaching, retreats and praying, good Christians and acts of kindness. Some things are separable: oil and water, Baptists and dancing, war and peace, teenagers and maturity, running and walking. For James, faith and deeds (or works) are as inseparable as children in a pool and splashing and diving and bobbing and laughing and teasing and blowing bubbles. Some in his world thought faith and works were as separable as silence and speech.

Some spoilsports think connecting works and faith misunderstands faith and risks salvation. Some are not spoilsports at all; they are profound theologians locked down on the work of Christ as absolutely sufficient. So, they want to assert we need to be careful here. They're right. I sometimes put it this way: we need both Dietrich

Bonhoeffer pleading for us to become fully devoted disciples (works), and we need Max Lucado reminding us over and over of God's utter love and grace and that trust is the ticket to God's presence (faith). But faith and works are not polar opposites; they are inseparable. Faith works, and works are faith in action, but they are not identical. Those who think they can achieve enough good works to merit acceptance with God will fail to find that acceptance because they confuse what works are all about.

James asks two pointed questions that show faith and works are inseparable:

> "What good is it?"
> "Can such a faith"—the kind of "faith" without
>   works—"save them"?

The answers are "No good!" and "No!" Genuine faith and good works are inseparable, not because works merit salvation, but because the good God who empowers us to good faith transforms us into doers of good works. This is why he says, "In the same way, faith by itself, if it is not accompanied by works, is dead" (2:17). This is not an either-or theory but a both-and lived theology. James presses questions upon his readers (then and now).

What good works does James have in mind? This discussion still creates chaos in some circles. Good works is a common practice among observant Jews who passed the practice on to the Christians, and this practice distinguished both Jews and Christians from both Greeks and Romans. The latter two groups had very little concern for the poor and starving. But from the beginning, Israelites were taught to care for the poor and especially for widows and orphans. Mercy, the most important term in the last line of the previous passage (2:13), was their term for what we call compassion and justice and social justice. Moses taught the people of Israel not to harvest the whole field and they formed a community of almsgiving as the safety net for the poor. (Mary, mother of James, by the way, was poor, and James had the status of an orphan.) So what James says is from the heart and body. Those without clothing and food are not to be wished away with some cavalier prayer or blessing (2:15–16). Nope, they are to be given clothing and food. That's what "good works" means for James: caring for the poor and marginalized. James may be looking at you and me asking, "How are you caring for the poor?"

But what about Paul? If you are thinking James is talking about Paul, you have something in your favor. Paul is the strongest proponent of justification by faith and not by works, and he writes it all up in Galatians and Romans. Still, James' description of what he is responding to is not exactly Paul, so it may be wisest to think James is responding to someone (The Proponent) who has taken Paul's teaching on faith alone to an extreme. Exciting ideas excite excitable disciples, and critics of excited disciples do their own bit of exaggerating too! So James digs in his heels. The Proponent, in 2:17, divides the terms and builds a wall between them: "One person has faith, and another person has works. What's the worry?!" Perhaps The Proponent had a kind of tolerant pluralism. James jumps up talking before he gets his hand in the air by appealing to their inseparability: "No way! You think you can show your faith

43

without works, but I show my faith by my works." Here's how silly their inseparability is: Good Jews believe there is one and only one God, but even demons believe that. It is not enough to believe the right things. Faith works itself out into works. They are that inseparable. Workless faith is not faith, and faithless works is also not faith.

Where did he come up with this inseparability idea? We must pause here to notice the *Shema* from Deuteronomy 6:4-9 again. It goes like this: "Hear O Israel, the Lord our God, the Lord is one." By way of reminder, a scribe asked Jesus which of the 613 commands was the most important, and Jesus said it was actually two: Love God (Deuteronomy 6:4-5) and love your neighbor as yourself (Lev. 19:18). James is the only book in the New Testament that mentions both loving God (James 1:12; 2:5) and loving others (2:8). So when James accuses The Proponent of believing that God is one, he's quoting again the *Shema*. The Proponent not only divides creed from practice (faith without works) but also loving God (Proponent's creed) from loving others (Jesus Creed). James got this idea from Jesus.

What about Abraham? James reacted in his day to what we today call "easy believism" or "cheap grace" or "salvation without discipleship" or "Jesus without the cross" or "victorious living without self-denial." These terms, too, are as inseparable as an engine and a car. To deepen his points, James trots out two noteworthy examples from the Bible in the good-working Abraham and Rahab. One man, one woman.

Abraham was "justified"—declared right, made right —"when he offered his son Isaac" (see Gen. 22:1–19) as a work that exhibited faith, and the two—his faith, his offering–brought his faith to its intended goal. Faith's goal is faith over and over, or faithfulness. His offering— that is, his work—completed the very act of faith God affirmed when Scripture said it was "credited to him as righteousness" (2:23). James aimed his words at the final line of the third paragraph of this section of his letter: "a person," you can see from this example of Abraham, "is justified *by works* and *not by faith alone*" (see 2:24). What James says here fits with how Jews of his day thought of Abraham's faith. In 1 Maccabees 2:51–52, it says, "Remember the deeds of the ancestors, which they did in their generations; and you will receive great honor and an everlasting name. Was not Abraham found faithful when tested, and it was reckoned to him as righteousness?" (NRSV) Jews did not distinguish the first act of faith from all other acts of faith but instead tied all acts of faith into a bundle called faithfulness or allegiance. Faith and works are distinguishable, but they are also inseparable. Now consider this. In Genesis 18, Abraham was hospitable to strangers, one of the preeminent acts of faith and good works in the Jewish world, and then he was tested in Genesis 22 to offer his son, and thus we could say his works of mercy were tested by God, and he proved faithful. Rahab's good work, too, is hospitality for people who were strangers to her.

Why Rahab? James' worry is the person who affirms faith without works. Faith alone is the person who sees the poor person and, instead of doing justice by providing food and clothing and shelter, wishes the person well. Connecting Abraham to Rahab from Joshua 6:16–25 may have stretched the sensibilities of some but not James: her work was the act of hospitality for the spies and her surreptitious plan for their escape. Again, James' goal is the last line. Just as a body without breath is dead, so a faith without works is a dead faith. He chooses Rahab because she, like Abraham, showed mercy to those in need. That's what faith is, and that's what works are. Choosing a woman turns toward us and asks our preachers today if their illustrations represent both sisters and brothers. Women then and women now are as full of works, if not more, as men. It's time for us to tell their stories, too.

So how important is this idea? James makes the very point four times:

1. faith without works of mercy is useless ("what good is it?"; 2:14, 16),
2. faith without works cannot save (2:14),
3. faith without works doesn't work (2:20, NIV has "useless"), and
4. faith without works is dead (2:17, 26).

How much more important can something be?!

The intent of this passage it not to make us feel good about our daily Bible reading or our church attendance but to push us to see that genuine faith prompts genuine concern for the needy we can help. Like the Parable of the Good Samaritan (Luke 10:25–37) and Jesus' constant concern for the sick and needy (Matthew 8:1–9:38), James knows that wise faith is merciful faith. Faith without mercy is not faith.

QUESTIONS FOR REFLECTION AND APPLICATION

1. What does "good works" mean to James?

2. McKnight suggests James is responding to a person he calls "The Proponent." How does imagining this passage as a dialogue shift your understanding of it?

3. Explain why James uses Abraham and Rahab as examples of faith-and-works faithfulness.

4. What are the four different ways James states his point?

5. What had you been taught about faith and works in church or Bible study previously? How has this interpretation from McKnight affected your understanding?

FOR FURTHER READING

Kent Annan, *Slow Kingdom Coming* (Downers Grove, IL: IVP Books, 2016).

Matthew Bates, *Gospel Allegiance* (Grand Rapids: Brazos, 2019).

Lynn Cohick, *Women in the World of the Earliest Christians* (Grand Rapids: Baker Academic, 2009).

Lynn Cohick and Amy Brown Hughes, *Christian Women in the Patristic World* (Grand Rapids: Baker Academic, 2017).

WISE WORDS

James 3:1–12

[1] *Not many of you should become teachers, my fellow believers, because you know that we who teach will be judged more strictly. [2] We all stumble in many ways. Anyone who is never at fault in what they say is perfect, able to keep their whole body in check.*

[3] *When we put bits into the mouths of horses to make them obey us, we can turn the whole animal. [4] Or take ships as an example. Although they are so large and are driven by strong winds, they are steered by a very small rudder wherever the pilot wants to go. [5] Likewise, the tongue is a small part of the body, but it makes great boasts. Consider what a great forest is set on fire by a small spark. [6] The tongue also is a fire, a world of evil among the parts of the body. It corrupts the whole body, sets the whole course of one's life on fire, and is itself set on fire by hell.*

[7] *All kinds of animals, birds, reptiles and sea creatures are being tamed and have been tamed by mankind, [8] but no human being can tame the tongue. It is a restless evil, full of deadly poison.*

[9] *With the tongue we praise our Lord and Father,*

and with it we curse human beings, who have been made in God's likeness. [10] Out of the same mouth come praise and cursing. My brothers and sisters, this should not be. [11] Can both fresh water and salt water flow from the same spring? [12] My brothers and sisters, can a fig tree bear olives, or a grapevine bear figs? Neither can a salt spring produce fresh water.

A scan of the New Testament letters reveals problems, problems, problems. In Galatia, some of the Jewish believers were convinced gentile believers were only partial converts until they completely embraced the law of Moses. Which would mean undergoing a very significant, if delicate, operation. You think it's hard to get men to church today? Try first-century Galatia! Paul wrote a letter to Corinth that is organized by questions about problems among Christians there. They had a personality cult problem; they had sex-with-a-family-member problem; they had worship problems; they had social status and power problems; they had theological problems; and they weren't all that hyped up about Paul collecting money for the poor in Jerusalem. In Colosse, there were evidently some folks worshiping angels or at least seeking ecstatic worship experiences.

My father was a model student in high school—smart, polite, student leader, college-bound. His younger brother was not. As my father told us over and over to our great delight, one of his brother's teachers asked him in class, "Bob, why can't you be like your brother, Junior?" To which my uncle, always game for a good time, said, "Because it takes all kinds to make up a world!" I think of my father's anecdote every time I read the New Testament letters—it takes all kinds, too, to make up a full list of church problems.

One of those problems—ever hear of this one?—was how they talked about one another. No book in the Bible talks more about speech problems than James, though the book of Proverbs sprints ahead at times for the shekels. Here are two examples.

> Those who guard their lips preserve their lives, but those who speak rashly will come to ruin (13:3).

> The tongue has the power of life and death, and those who love it will eat its fruit (18:21).

Jesus, too, warned about the use of the tongue. He told his followers that "what comes out of a person [spoken words] is what defiles them" (Mark 7:20), and he was strong in words about those labeling and slandering others (Matt. 5:21–22). As you read James, notice how often James brings up speech ethics. There are thirty-two imperatives in this short letter, twenty-nine of which are about speech! He's already given us a small basket of suggestions (1:19–20; 2:2–4; 2:12; 2:16), but in chapters three through four he gives us a barrel full of wisdom about speech.

James contributes wisdom about speech because his churches had some lippy problems.

So do we. Social media reveals our problems, and at least four serious problems for all of us are splashing around on the surface of our social media. First, we are developing a diminished capacity for genuine conversation. One

51

researcher reports that empathy has receded 40 percent among college students and that more and more families eat dinner together with a device next to the plate (Turkle).

Second, we are being influenced or formed and perhaps controlled by the bots. The algorithms in our social media—Facebook, Instagram, Twitter, whatever—are designed for each person according to what each person spends time reading and watching. Those algorithms are more interested in what gets you riled up than what makes you serene and happy. It all tilts in the direction of your ire and temptation to make snarky remarks. More money goes to the social media company the more irritated you become (Lanier).

Third, two researchers recently have shown that social media especially capitalizes on our desire to be recognized as important by coaxing us into "grandstanding expressions" that gain affirmations through "likes," emojis, and reactions. Further, this grandstanding phenomenon tempts us to pile on others in disapproval (and so feel good about our moral perceptions), to ramp up what others have said and then to express the strongest forms of outrage and joy in the process (Tosi and Warmke). All this, to repeat the second observation, appears on our screen because of bots.

Fourth, the digital world is disembodied interaction, and we are embodied people who need the presence of other bodies to be who we are designed by God to be. Disembodied people don't behave as well as when they are with others (Kim).

James just got real. A man from the first century writing to Christians in exile just found time-travel binoculars powerful enough to see through our speech into our hearts. What can we learn from what he says in our passage about how to talk to one another and how to use our social media?

First, James seems quite interested in teachers (3:1), and he wants those desiring to be speakers and teachers to weigh the implications. Words matter. Teachers matter, too, as their words and ideas ripple from one person to another and from those on to other generations. Teachers use words that can heal and words that can destroy. Everybody who doesn't teach is now eyeballing the room for teachers, and some have a bit of glee in their eyes. But don't start pointing fingers at me just yet! One can easily recognize that these words pertain to anyone speaking words of influence, from teachers and pastors and political leaders to mothers and fathers and siblings and neighbors and coaches. Anyone speaking is in mind and here's the download, heavier than you may expect: *speech measures maturity*. "Anyone who is never at fault in what they say is perfect" (3:2). Mature persons control the tongue. We need wisdom.

Second, *speech has an impact that far exceeds its size*. Words have wings, as Homer and Plutarch both said. A bit in the bridle can be used to lead a horse, a small rudder steers even a large boat, and the tongue has the same kind of excessive impact. James says, "the tongue is a small member, yet it boasts of great exploits" (see 3:5, the final word in 3:3–5). Speaking of impact, images created through words have a lasting power, and James uses images in abundance in our passage. (You can think separately about each one.) Boasting surprises us on first reading. Maybe we should have seen boasting in the word "humbly" in 1:21 or the "tight rein on their tongues" in 1:26 and in 3:1's concern with too many wanting to be teachers. Other passages in James will suggest that some are using their tongues for boasting, but 3:14 mentions it directly. Let's just call it "grandstanding" or its close friend "virtue signaling," and we are up to date. The little tongue has enormous reach and when parents present nasty speech habits in the family, when teachers do the same in classrooms, when pastors get bombastic in the pulpit, and when neighbors decide to pound on others, a culture of criticism forms that turns humans against one another. This creates tribes of people. Social media, too, is a small platform with more than enormous reach. It boggles.

Third, *speech, like fire and poison, can destroy and kill.* We only need to read James' words here and think of how they play out in our world, not just on social media but in our churches as well. Speech is a "fire" and "a world of evil" and it "corrupts the whole body" and—no fear of exaggeration for James!—"sets the whole course of one's life on fire" and is "itself set on fire by hell" (3:6). He's not done yet. It is a "restless evil, full of deadly poison" (3:8). We use it to degrade humans, and we use it to praise God. Pick your image, it's full of potential (3:11–12). Those speaking into the lives of others can guide them into darkness; they can slander others; they can humiliate others; and they can assert their own power. Or they can heal and comfort and toss grace back and forth, word by word.

One thing is clear in James: the man's a realist. For him, fourth, *speech seems to be uncontrollable.* This theme is found in a sudden burst of exasperation in James 3:7–8 and is stated in comprehensive terms: "no human being can tame the tongue" even though we can tame the animal kingdom. Yet, the one who controls the tongue is approved (1:26; 3:2). Sirach, a wisdom writer in James' Jewish world, said, "If you blow on a spark, it will glow; if you spit on it, it will be put out; yet both come out of your mouth" (28:12). Not the same, but close enough to bring the message home.

How do we put this together? Speech is the far frontier and fiercest opponent in the fight to subdue sin. James wants everyone who uses the keyboard to know that what we write comes from the heart, and he wants hearts sold out in a way that glorify God—word by word.

QUESTIONS FOR REFLECTION AND APPLICATION

1. Why do the words of teachers (and anyone speaking) matter so much?

2. Which of James' word pictures about speech do you most relate to, and why?

3. How do James' imperatives about speech ethics cause you to pause before you speak?

4. Which of the four serious problems of social media conversation that McKnight lays out impacts your own communication most? Diminished capacity for conversation, bot-controlled content that feeds on irritation, a desire to be recognized as important, or piling on others in disapproval? Why?

5. What will you do with your words this week to spread grace and not fire? Be specific with examples.

FOR FURTHER READING

William Baker, *Sticks and Stones: The Discipleship of Our Speech* (Downers Grove, IL: IVP, 1996).

Jay Y. Kim, *Analog Church: Why We Need Real People, Places, and Things in the Digital Age* (Downers Grove, IL: IVP, 2020).

Jaron Lanier, *Ten Arguments for Deleting Your Social Media Accounts Right Now* (New York: Picador, 2019).

Scot McKnight, "Wise Speech," in eds. Scot McKnight, Daniel J. Hanlon, *Wise Church: Forming a Wisdom Culture in Your Local Church* (Eugene, OR: Cascade, 2021), 248–273.

Beth Moore, with Melissa Moore, *James: Mercy Triumphs* (Nashville: LifeWay, 2011).

Plutarch, *Concerning Talkativeness*.

Justin Tosi, Brandon Warmke, *Grandstanding: The Use and Abuse of Moral Talk* (New York: Oxford, 2020).

Sherry Turkle, *Reclaiming Conversation: The Power of Talk in a Digital Age* (New York: Penguin, 2015).

WISE WISDOM

James 3:13-18

¹³ *Who is wise and understanding among you? Let them show it by their good life, by works* done in the humility that comes from wisdom.*

¹⁴ *But if you harbor bitter envy and selfish ambition in your hearts, do not boast about it or deny the truth.* ¹⁵ *Such "wisdom" does not come down from heaven but is earthly, unspiritual, demonic.* ¹⁶ *For where you have envy and selfish ambition, there you find disorder and every evil practice.*

¹⁷ *But the wisdom that comes from heaven is first of all pure; then peace-loving, considerate, submissive, full of mercy and good fruit, impartial and sincere.* ¹⁸ *Peacemakers who sow in peace reap a harvest of righteousness.*

*See my comments on the term "works" in the footnote on p. 40.

Not all wisdoms are wise, so let's work on getting a solid grip on the meaning of wisdom. Our modern USA and our modern church life are not wisdom cultures. Instead, we have an information culture shaped more by trends and fads than by the wisdom of sages. In other cultures even today, young people want to grow up to be like the bald-headed and gray-haired, while in our culture, the older people want to be like the young. Ellen Davis, a scholar of the wisdom books of the Old Testament, including Proverbs, said wisdom is "living in the world in such a way that God, and God's intentions for the world, are acknowledged in all that we do," and she observes this derives not from innate intelligence or the cultivation of education, but it derives from a life lived wholly before God. Those dedicated to becoming wise are not in the ambitious quest for power but for goodness. So, let's summarize this by saying wisdom is *living in God's world in God's way.* It takes time—a lifetime—to become wise.

There's more. Wisdom is a skill acquired by those who listen to the wise, and Proverbs 1:1–7 shows that a budding wise person reverently listens to and receives the wisdom that drips from sages. To grow in wisdom requires that kind of posture: one who listens to the wise and heeds their wisdom. If you want to grow in wisdom, the first step is to find someone who is already wise, the second is for that person to become a presence in your life, and the third is to live in a way consistent with that wisdom. Even more, if wisdom is living in God's world in God's way, and if God's way is that Christ is our wisdom (1 Cor. 1:30; Col. 2:3; Hanlon), then true wisdom is living in God's world by living in *the way of Christ.*

Some "wisdom" is Christlike and some is not. In fact, the NIV's choice to translate such wisdom with scare quotes, as "wisdom," pins the nose of the problem to the wall. Reckless wisdom blurts from the mouth of fools, of the angry, of the violent, and of the powerful. Notice the words James uses for reckless wisdom: "bitter envy" and "selfish ambition" and "boast" and "deny the truth" (3:14). These are the habits that ruin community life. (Have you ever observed how many of the ethical categories in the New Testament have to do with our life together?) As wise wisdom comes to us through Christ, reckless wisdom is "earthly, unspiritual, demonic" (3:15), and one can't find three terms any stronger than these. Put differently: of the world, not from the Spirit, and devilish. Reckless wisdom corrupts community life through its bad habits and so it leads to anarchy and "every evil practice" (3:16). Disorder, anarchy, and confusion are the signals of reckless wisdom.

Wise teachers are described by James in 3:13 and in 3:17–18. Here are the habits that form them into being wise in their inmost character. First, there's a triad of connections: their "works," or acts of compassion and justice toward those in need, are done in wisdom's "humility," and here humility counters the boasting of the reckless ones. Wisdom's humble works come from their "excellent conduct of life" (3:13, my translation). Second, James, knowing that we can all tell anecdotes of each, instead lists eight habits of a wise character (3:17, my translation):

- devout,
- peaceful,
- gentle,
- persuadable,
- full of compassion and good fruits,
- non-biased,
- not fraudulent.

Recall from James chapters one and two the tensions, the anger, and the careless labels being used by some for others in the community. So much tension was in play, and he's got his eyes fixed on the teachers especially, that he has to pause to talk speech patterns. Now he's filling it all out with a list of virtues for a person with wise character. Bible readers fall too easily into turning lists like these into a list of qualifications, and before long they become a morality checklist that tortures those among us who have overly scrupulous consciences. Such persons ask, "Was I gentle enough there [no] or am I too unpersuadable [yes] or am I a big fraud [am I?]?" No, this mistakes the list. These are manifestations—what James calls in the next verse "harvest" or better yet "fruit." Fruits grow on trees, and good trees, Jesus said, produce good fruit (Matt. 7:16–20). So these are not designed for a checklist, but they are designed for you and me to ask if we have the kind of character (tree)—one filled with the Spirit, shaped by God's grace, determined by presence with Jesus as the Sage of all sages—that produces this kind of fruit.

Take this all into your church and right inside your own home: if we use our social media, if we talk with one another, and if we teach and preach with these eight terms in mind, we will end up right where James does, with one of the most beautiful verses in the Bible: "Peacemakers who sow in peace reap a harvest [or fruit] of righteousness" (3:18). James creates here a beautiful circular statement: those who want peace plant the seeds of peace—of course they do—and the fruit turns out right (which means the fruit is a just peace). Peace all over the place. Peace can be the umpire for all our relationships in a church.

Wise wisdom forms into a character that turns community life into peaceful relationships. Reckless wisdom prefers chaos. We end where James began: "Who is wise and understanding among you?"

QUESTIONS FOR REFLECTION AND APPLICATION

1. What does McKnight mean by "not all wisdoms are wise"?

2. What are the differences between Christlike wisdom and reckless wisdom?

3. How does McKnight translate James' eight habits of Christlike character?

4. Which of those traits do you see present in your life, as you examine the "fruit" growing from your "tree"?

5. McKnight says the steps to wisdom are: "find someone who is already wise . . . for that person to become a presence in your life, and . . . to live in a way consistent with that wisdom." Think of a wise person you want to become more like. Where are you in that process of gaining from their wisdom? What will you do to move to the next step?

FOR FURTHER READING

Ellen F. Davis, *Proverbs, Ecclesiastes, and the Song of Songs*, Westminster Bible Companion (Louisville: Westminster John Knox, 2000), 1, 27.

Daniel J. Hanson, "What Is Wisdom?" in eds. Scot McKnight, Daniel J. Hanlon, *Wise Church: Forming a Wisdom Culture in Your Local Church* (Eugene, OR: Cascade, 2021), 1–24.

Mandy Smith, *The Vulnerable Pastor* (Downers Grove, IL: IVP Books, 2015).

WISE POWER

James 4:1-12

¹ What causes fights and quarrels among you? Don't they come from your desires that battle within you? ² You desire but do not have, so you kill. You covet but you cannot get what you want, so you quarrel and fight. You do not have because you do not ask God. ³ When you ask, you do not receive, because you ask with wrong motives, that you may spend what you get on your pleasures.

⁴ You adulterous people, don't you know that friendship with the world means enmity against God? Therefore, anyone who chooses to be a friend of the world becomes an enemy of God. ⁵ Or do you think Scripture says without reason that he jealously longs for the spirit he has caused to dwell in us? ⁶ But he gives us more grace. That is why Scripture says:

"God opposes the proud

but shows favor to the humble."

⁷ Submit yourselves, then, to God. Resist the devil, and he will flee from you. ⁸ Come near to God and he will come near to you. Wash your hands, you sinners, and purify your hearts, you double-minded. ⁹ Grieve, mourn and wail.

Change your laughter to mourning and your joy to gloom.
¹⁰ Humble yourselves before the Lord, and he will lift you up.
¹¹ Brothers and sisters, do not slander one another.
Anyone who speaks against a brother or sister or judg-
es them speaks against the law and judges it. When you
judge the law, you are not keeping it, but sitting in judg-
ment on it. ¹² There is only one Lawgiver and Judge, the
one who is able to save and destroy. But you—who are
you to judge your neighbor?

The man who told us to be careful with how we talk to one another let it rip in these verses. Abusing power earns James' strongest language. Lurking on the margins of the three chapters we have already studied in James have been some power-mongering hotheads who abused with their tongues. Angry words (1:19–21), hypocritical words (1:26), degrading words (2:3–4), words without empathy (2:16), and chaos-causing words (3:1–12) are swirling in the air by the time we encounter the power-mongering words found in James 4:1–12. James has had it, so he lets it rip.

What's happening in these churches? "Fights and quarrels" explode from the battles in their "desires" (4:1). So strong is that desire to dominate that he says "so you kill" (4:2). I'm not the only person who wonders if James speaks here of the Zealot-types who actually maimed and even murdered those deemed unfaithful. Their "coveting" led to their warring with one another (4:2). Their lack of character doesn't stop them from asking God to give them their desires—God's not party to them because they are in it for "pleasures" (4:3). Their problem of pride (4:6) comes from the devil (4:7), they are (again) "double-minded" (4:8), and they spill out words of slander and condemnation on one another (4:11–12). Because my daughter (Laura Barringer) and I wrote a book that discussed toxic cultures in churches, we both get too many letters from people, many of them associate pastors, wounded by abusive senior pastors. Sometimes my wife, Kris, after either reading the letters or hearing one of us describe one, blurts out, "What's going on? This shouldn't happen in churches!" I wonder if we shouldn't ask, "What in *hell* is going on in the church?" James would say this stuff comes from the pit of hell!

We have a word for the ambitious, power-mongering, self-centered, and pleasure-seeking person: narcissist. An English professor, Steve Taylor, sketched this all-too-common human problem with such succinct words he has to be quoted:

> One of the human race's biggest problems has been that people who occupy positions of power are often incapable of using power in a responsible way. . . . in more recent times, it seems as though power attracts ruthless and narcissistic people with a severe lack of empathy and conscience. . . . People with these personalities can't sense other people's feelings or see the world from any perspective apart from their own. They don't have a sense of conscience or guilt to stop them behaving immorally. They feel superior and enjoy manipulating and controlling other people. At the same time, they need to feel respected and admired and like to be the centre of attention. . . . Research, for example, shows

that people with narcissistic and psychopathic traits have a strong desire for dominance and are disproportionately common in leadership positions.

James didn't call them narcissists, but our word fits his descriptions. Such persons are given to grandiosity, they must be admired, they ruin relationships (James 3:1–12 and 4:1–12), they are offended by the slightest of suggestions, and they have no empathy for others. In the last month, I've received two long letters from associate pastors telling a story of being fired for simple questions for the pastor. One man said his fault was told to him by the church leaders in these words: "I had questioned the leadership and that would not be tolerated." It happened then, and it happens now: ambitious, power-seeking leaders will find positions where they can exert power. Challenging them, however biblical and morally good, leads too often to the abuse of power and especially to attacking people by name-calling, gaslighting, discrediting and demonizing, spinning the story, silencing, bribing through Non-Disclosure Agreements (called generous severance packages), suppressing the truth, and faking apologies.

Wise power is not like this. Power is a powder keg, and the more respectful we are of it, the better off we are. When handled with wisdom, power becomes power *for* and power *with* and not power *over*. Power *for* empowers others; power *with* shares power; power *over* dominates others. The first two make a person a "friend of God," while the third turns a person into a friend of the world and an enemy of

God (4:4–5). Jesus had told his closest followers the way of Rome (the way of the world) was all about power, prestige, celebrity, and abuse. In that context, he told them his way was the way of serving others—power *for* and *with* (Mark 10:34–45).

Friendship was a top dinner table conversation in James' world. Aristotle wrote a whole book about friendship and then the Roman orator Cicero did the same. To suggest people would be friends with God, though, was rather extraordinary. How does James instruct us in this kind of friendship with God, the way of wise power? *Grace transforms our desire for power.* Bible scholars pitch a fit every time they read James 4:5–6 because, well, there are some confusing expressions. Here is my own translation:

> [5] Or, do you think that the writing hollowly says, "The spirit that resides in us longs toward envy?" [6] But [God] gives greater grace. Because it says, God resists the status-mongers but gives grace to the impoverished ones [Proverbs 3:34].

I will attempt to paraphrase all this now. Humans have ambitious desires for power (James 4:1–4). That is, the selfish spirit within them envies others, but God can change humans so God gives grace. That is what Proverbs 3:34 more or less also says, only in quoting Scripture James adds an important point—"to the impoverished ones." This translation combines the poverty theme of this book with the powermonger's use of abusive words. They are the target of these abuses of power. But these powermongers can be transformed from angry, word-spewing judges into power-for and power-with leaders if they humble themselves before God.

That God is a God of grace. Grace, what a word! A gift given, which is what grace means, binds the Giver to the Receiver, and—don't let this slip from your mind—obligates the Receiver to express gratitude and allegiance and even to reciprocate as one can. In God's granting us the gift of forgiveness, we experience God's initiating superabundant love that overcomes our undeservedness of that gift. Yet, in that gift, God becomes present to us. Our gracious God's presence transforms us into gift-givers ourselves. Let's cut straight across the track to the finish line—which means, unlike the power leaders in James' churches, we should not verbally, physically, and sexually abuse others! Especially the poor, who are now nodding their heads in approval.

God favors the humble. Because James knows it needs emphasis, he sets out a string of commands for these status-mongering, power-abusing leaders, each of which is nothing less than an expression of confession of their sin, repentance for their ways, and a step in a new direction of wise power. They are to submit to God, resist the devil, draw near to God, cleanse their hands, purify their hearts, lament, mourn, weep, reject their hilarity and joys and—back to the last words of Proverbs 3:34—to humble themselves (or impoverish themselves). Please don't take these as scrupulous separable commands and then try to do each one. Instead, this is a barrage of terms all saying the same thing: repent from your ways and turn to God.

God's grace swarms to transform. That's what James wants us to hear.

Abusers of powers find their way into leadership. These, sad to say, are words of a "pastor" I recently read on Twitter who was criticizing a book by a wonderful scholar, and this is what he said of her: that she "is not a Christian right? She affirms the blaspheming of marriage and the destruction of souls it produces. I ask you because you seem to be interacting with her as a sister rather than a wolf." These words are a sad example of what we discussed about social media at James 3:1–12. They are also the height of arrogance because this person has publicly condemned another Christian. That's not his calling at all; that's God's. He usurped the work of God. No words applied more to the leaders of James' churches or to this kind of public accusation than what James says in 4:11–12. What he says is that God, the *Judge, and God alone makes these decisions.* A wide gap stands between preaching the gospel and taking the place of God. Narcissists, with their expanded ego, leap the gap and stand in for God. Another command to complement the humbling of 4:7–10 is "do not slander one another" and don't "speak against" one's Christian siblings and don't "judge" others. To judge another is to condemn another person as if one were God, as if one were the Lawgiver himself!

Wise power surrenders to God what God does and submits to God to do what God wants. Perhaps we could paraphrase the last line of our passage with this: Who do you think you are!?!

QUESTIONS FOR REFLECTION
AND APPLICATION

1. Can you think of a power-mongering Christian leader in your life or one you have heard about? How does their behavior compare to what James describes in this passage?

2. What are the differences among power *for*, power *with*, and power *over*?

3. How does McKnight explain the kind of grace that transforms our desire for power?

4. Do you need to take any of the actions James sets out for people who ought to humble themselves? Which ones? What would that look like in your life?

5. Have you been harmed by a narcissistic church leader or other authority figure, or do you know someone who has? How can this lesson help you recognize that misrepresentation of God or bring healing from God to your heart?

FOR FURTHER READING

John Barclay, *Paul and the Gift* (Grand Rapids: Wm. B. Eerdmans, 2015).

Twitter: @lambeth981 (Matt Kennedy), first week of April 2021.

Scot McKnight, Laura Barringer, *A Church Called Tov: Forming a Goodness Culture That Resists Abuses of Power and Promotes Healing* (Carol Stream, IL: Tyndale Momentum, 2020), 25–39.

Steve Taylor, a lecturer in psychology at Leeds Beckett University: https://theconversation.com/how-to-stop-psychopaths-and-narcissists-from-winning-positions-of-power-158183

WISE BUSINESS

James 4:13–5:11

[13] Now listen, you who say, "Today or tomorrow we will go to this or that city, spend a year there, carry on business and make money." [14] Why, you do not even know what will happen tomorrow. What is your life? You are a mist that appears for a little while and then vanishes. [15] Instead, you ought to say, "If it is the Lord's will, we will live and do this or that." [16] As it is, you boast in your arrogant schemes. All such boasting is evil. [17] If anyone, then, knows the good they ought to do and doesn't do it, it is sin for them.

[5:1] Now listen, you rich people, weep and wail because of the misery that is coming on you. [2] Your wealth has rotted, and moths have eaten your clothes. [3] Your gold and silver are corroded. Their corrosion will testify against you and eat your flesh like fire. You have hoarded wealth in the last days. [4] Look! The wages you failed to pay the workers who mowed your fields are crying out against you. The cries of the harvesters have reached the ears of the Lord Almighty. [5] You have lived on earth in luxury and self-indulgence. You have fattened yourselves in the day of

slaughter. ⁶ *You have condemned and murdered the inno-*
cent one, who was not opposing you.

⁷ *Be patient, then, brothers and sisters, until the Lord's*
coming. See how the farmer waits for the land to yield its
valuable crop, patiently waiting for the autumn and spring
rains. ⁸ *You too, be patient and stand firm, because the*
Lord's coming is near. ⁹ *Don't grumble against one another,*
brothers and sisters, or you will be judged. The Judge is
standing at the door! ¹⁰ *Brothers and sisters, as an example*
of patience in the face of suffering, take the prophets who
spoke in the name of the Lord. ¹¹ *As you know, we count as*
blessed those who have persevered. You have heard of Job's
perseverance and have seen what the Lord finally brought
about. The Lord is full of compassion and mercy.

Wisdom and wealth have a conflicted relationship.
The Bible teaches that the obedient and wise can
be wealthy while the riches of the disobedient and foolish
may go up in smoke (Deut. 28). That some Israelites were
"successful" enough to become extravagant consumerists
and others entrenched in generational poverty led Moses
to institute policies like the Year of Jubilee (Lev. 25) and
gleaning (19:9–10). Hard work, which wisdom extols
(Prov. 20:13), can be erased by injustice and oppression
(13:23), sometimes at the hands of Israel's leaders who
are called to protect the poor (Isa. 58). The tragic story of
Job shows that obedience and blessing can become flipped
scripts. This conflicted relationship—sometimes a divine
blessing and at other times the excesses of exploitation—
forms the realities of early Christian perceptions of wealth,
too. Some obedient ones are poor, some are wealthy; some

disobedient are poor, some are wealthy. Jesus, standing in one corner of this conflict, blessed the poor and uttered a loud Oy! to the wealthy (Luke 6:20–26). Jesus, like James, favored the poor (1:26–27; 2:1–12; 5:1–6).

Wisdom discerns the difference. Wisdom itself is a kind of wealth according to Proverbs 3:13–14: "Blessed are those who find wisdom . . . for she is more profitable than silver and yields better returns than gold." These lines in Proverbs reveal how wisdom relativizes wealth by making true wealth wisdom itself. As Brandon Evans puts it, "Material wealth may be acquired with wisdom. But wisdom can *never* be acquired with money." Neither can spiritual gifts be purchased, and too many today buy power and influence and inner-circle presence with their wealth. James pointed a long finger at such practices.

James instructs us that wise business, when defined as living in God's world in the way of Christ, requires two habits: trusting God and paying just wages. Both passages begin with a tip-off that heated words are on their way: "Now listen!" This little expression launches James into warnings about reckless business practices. Negative examples frequently provide positive instruction. James may be speaking about unbelieving merchants and farmers. If so, he's more concerned with believing merchants, and he provides for them two wise habits.

Two Wise Business Habits

Plan under the guidance of God. The merchant on the move for profits talks arrogantly, and I paraphrase James:

75

"Soon we will go to this port, and we'll spend a long time there doing our business and we'll make some good profits" (4:13). As one nurtured in the Bible's wisdom about work, industriousness, and discipline, James was not one bit against working or planning. He's against arrogance. He knows Jeremiah from his youth: "Lord, I know that people's lives are not their own; it is not for them to direct their steps" (10:23). Proverbs too: "The human mind plans the way, but the Lord directs the steps" (16:9). These merchants arrogantly assumed their future and their profits.

One of the best methods of teaching is to ask good questions, even if sometimes they have an agenda behind them. Greek does not have question marks, so one has to discern questions from statements, and the NIV has two questions while the NRSV and CEB have but one ("What is your life?"). I'm with the NRSV and CEB on this one, so here's my version: "Whoever [you are], You don't know Tomorrow. What is your life? For you are a mist appearing for a little while, and then disappearing." That one question, even if the NIV makes it two, is powerful. It's a combination of "Who in the world do you think you are?" with "Do you think you are sovereign in life?" James wants to yank these merchants from a world in which they think they are its center into a divine world where they are but a speck visible for a moment. I'm thinking he got their attention as he gets mine.

In 2 Timothy, the apostle Paul says Scripture does four things: teaches, rebukes, corrects, and instructs us to walk on the right path (3:16–17). James illustrates that very approach in our passage. He gains attention, he asks questions as his form of rebuke, and he instructs them by way of correction and pointing the path forward.

Your life can be short.
Tomorrow is not guaranteed.
Life is comparable to mist.

So, you ought to be in prayer in the posture of trust and discernment instead of making plans with utter certainty. His corrections continue as he accuses them of boasting and arrogance (3:17).

His instruction follows. Those knowing what is good are to do it. How? One is to spend time in prayer communing with God, spend time in Scripture listening to God, and spend time in fellowship with others—merchants as well as mentors and fellow believers—discerning plans. The Lord's guidance requires fine-tuning in the ear, but those who go to the Lord over time recognize the voice of God. There is a fine line between planning in the posture of prayer and planning in the posture of presumption. The arrogant cross the line unknowingly while the wise businessperson fears that line.

These words shaped early Christians as they baptized business in the waters of Christ's lordship, and we dare not forget how challenging this was. Still is, in fact. Converted business leaders often find their business the most challenging place for living out the way of Christ. It is much easier to put the Christian life in the church-home network and to continue living as they did in the work-friends network. In a stimulating look at wisdom in the workplace, William Shiell summed it up: these early Christians "begin to see Christ as owner and their role as steward of the company" who are now "entrusted with workers who are equally valued as 'coworkers.'"

Pay your employees a just wage. The tone in James 5:1 sharpens. You may recall that James and his mother and brothers and sisters were poor, and they knew what it meant to receive from the generosity of others (1:27). Exploitation lurks behind James 5:1–6 as a family experience. We might begin best with verse four's accusation: the rich farmers were not paying their workers their wages. Some day laborers offered their services at farms in the morning, and Jesus told a parable about it (Matt. 20:1–16). Such persons often lived hand to mouth. Some wealthy farmers delayed their wages, resulting in the poor's pleas with God (James 5:4).

James turns to the wealthy with strong words: "Buckle up, because bad days are on your horizon! Your wealth rots, moths eat your clothing, and your money corrodes. Hoarding is not divine wisdom." But he's not done, so let's continue. The oppressed speak up in exasperated accusations that become pleas for God's justice to roll down upon the exploiters. Their luxurious life fattened up from the bank of hoarding will be met by a God named Justice! Millions today are uttering such pleas to God because of exploiting employers.

Paying people is just; paying them on time is just; paying them a just wage is even just-er. James does not here engage how much to pay a person, but today's readers need to think about it. The workers in this text, when not paid, starved. The Roman empire did not care about the starving poor. Jews and Christians did. James will not tolerate a Christian who has no empathy for the exploited poor. A Christian employer determines a wage, not by the market, but by the way of Christ. He or she does not ask, "How little do we have to pay this person?" Nor is the question "What do other employers pay?" They ask, "What is right? What is just? What empowers this person to be all this person can be?" Wise Christians work to diminish the excessive profits of exploiters.

This sharp-edged warning to the wealthy ends with questions for close readers. He says the wealthy "condemned and murdered the innocent one" and that the innocent person "was not opposing you." Who is this innocent person? We start with some wisdom—we can't be certain. There are three really good options, all based on the importance of righteousness words in James (1:20; 2:21–25; 3:18; and 5:16). Some think the person is Jesus, who is called the Righteous One (Acts 3:14). Some think this book was edited after James died and this refers to him, who was often called "James the Just [= righteous, innocent]" and to his martyrdom. Others think the singular—righteous one—represents plurally all the believers who are walking in the way of Jesus and suffering for it. I think this last view is best because James nuances his tenses in this passage. Only two verbs—"are crying out" and "not opposing you"—are in the present tense, a tense that puts something center stage. James wants his readers to hear the cries and to feel the powerlessness of the unpaid workers, so he pulls these verbs to the front of the stage.

He moves now to what many might think is a random change of topics. We will need to get back into James' world to understand what he says. Our response to unpaid workers might be, "Change the law. Vote in a better candidate. Boycott!" Those were not options in James' world. At times one little word can clarify what at first appeared to be a general statement. James' wisdom for the oppressed workers is to understand *patience as an exercise in plotting*. "Be patient," he says in 5:7, and we may well ask, "About what?" James tells us in verse ten. They are looking into the "face of suffering." He advocates a tactic: patience awaiting the day of justice, which in verse five he graphically named "the day of slaughter." Examples work for all of us, so James says the prophets were patient in their suffering. He could be talking about Jeremiah, Isaiah, or Daniel. Or he could be doing the very common thing of connecting prophets in general to suffering. Or maybe he wants us his readers to let our imaginations soar to the prophets that come to mind. Job, too, was for them another example, and he has been for many Christians and Jews since.

Let's back off this to see what's in view. If we don't, we could quickly use a good teaching in a bad situation. James speaks to poor day laborers who have no recourse to the courts and who are defrauded in pay. He has said the representative poor worker is not fighting back (5:6), he now says they are to be patient, he urges them not to gripe about one another, and he finds examples of patient resilience under suffering. This indicates clearly that the sufferer can do nothing about it. When you can do nothing about it, you cry out to God, and you wait for God's judgment to come down. This reminds me of the Spirituals of America's black slaves who, because they were degraded by the law as only 3/5ths of a person, had (seemingly) no recourse. So what did they do? They prayed. They sang songs we call Spirituals, and their songs included subtle coded words that expressed their anger and their hope that they'd cross the River Jordan, which was for many of them the Ohio River. Once over, they were free. An exhortation to patience like this one in James, I am suggesting, could be coded language as well for "do what you can when you can." As James considered the prophets "blessed," and as we all know "what the Lord finally brought about" for Job, so we know that someday, on the other side of the river, justice and freedom await because God will make all things right. And maybe in the meantime some will find liberation. Here is such a set of lines:

> *Slav'ry chain done broke at las'—*
> *Goin' to praise God 'til I die. . . .*
> *I did know my Jesus heard me*
> *'Cause de spirit spoke to me*
> *An' said, "Rise, my chile, your chillum,*
> *An' you too, shall be free!"*

Don't be surprised, then, if patience is coded language for "let's make it happen (tonight)!"

QUESTIONS FOR REFLECTION AND APPLICATION

1. Why do "wisdom and wealth have a conflicted relationship"? What are some of the points of conflict between them?

2. James instructs us that wise business (defined as living in God's world in the way of Christ) requires two habits: trusting God in planning and paying just wages. Which of these habits is more of a challenge in your life, and how does it affect you?

3. James teaches that those who know what is good are to do that good. What are three ways McKnight suggests we can follow that teaching?

4. McKnight offers a series of questions for Christian employers to ask themselves as they determine just wages for their employees. If you are an employer, how would it impact your life to ask and answer these questions? If you are an employee, how would it impact your life if your employer began asking these questions?

5. What would it look like for you to practice patience in suffering "as an exercise in plotting"? What would it change for you if your patience included planning to take what action you could?

FOR FURTHER READING

https://www.archives.gov/exhibits/documented-rights/exhibit/section2/detail/broke-at-last-lyrics.html

Brandon Evans, "Wise Church Economies," in eds. Scot McKnight, Daniel J. Hanlon, *Wise Church: Forming a Wisdom Culture in Your Local Church* (Eugene, OR: Cascade, 2021), 107–129.

William Shiell, "Wisdom in the Workplace," in eds. Scot McKnight, Daniel J. Hanlon, *Wise Church: Forming a Wisdom Culture in Your Local Church* (Eugene, OR: Cascade, 2021), 47–67.

Howard Thurman, *Deep River and the Negro Spiritual Speaks of Life and Death* (Richmond, IN: Friends United Press, 1990), 30.

WISE INSTRUCTIONS

James 5:12–20

¹² *Above all, my brothers and sisters, do not swear—not by heaven or by earth or by anything else. All you need to say is a simple "Yes" or "No." Otherwise you will be condemned.*

¹³ *Is anyone among you in trouble? Let them pray. Is anyone happy? Let them sing songs of praise.* ¹⁴ *Is anyone among you sick? Let them call the elders of the church to pray over them and anoint them with oil in the name of the Lord.* ¹⁵ *And the prayer offered in faith will make the sick person well; the Lord will raise them up. If they have sinned, they will be forgiven.* ¹⁶ *Therefore confess your sins to each other and pray for each other so that you may be healed. The prayer of a righteous person is powerful and effective.*

¹⁷ *Elijah was a human being, even as we are. He prayed earnestly that it would not rain, and it did not rain on the land for three and a half years.* ¹⁸ *Again he prayed, and the heavens gave rain, and the earth produced its crops.*

¹⁹ *My brothers and sisters, if one of you should wander from the truth and someone should bring that person back,*

²⁰ *remember this: Whoever turns a sinner from the error of their way will save them from death and cover over a multitude of sins.*

James ends with a random list of wise instructions. Random is fine—maybe James was running out of papyrus! He concludes his letter with three separable instructions: truth-telling not swearing, praying for those who are ill, and rescuing the wandering. Clever folks can try to bring them into some coherent unity, but what gives coherence here is that James is a pastor, and these are concerns in the churches to whom he writes. These instructions are a bit like reading a church's website. If you click a few levels down, you may find position papers about topics that are both important to that church and random in appearance. Different Christians need different instructions.

Christians need to tell the truth. That James starts with "Above all" surprises. Why is oath-making now suddenly the most important thing he has to say, and if it is so important, why wait until now, and then, also, if it is "above all," why only one verse? Instead of reading too much into "above all," we are wise to understand this as a cliché for "finally."

There is something very special about James that I have refrained from discussing openly until now: no book after the four Gospels sounds more like Jesus than James. Read it sometime and notice how often he echoes sayings of Jesus. But James has not yet quoted Jesus once! Until this verse. The ability to sound like Jesus without ever quoting him reveals that this younger brother of Jesus had so absorbed his Messiah's teachings that he could not talk without sounding like Jesus. I can think of no higher compliment to our author than this: You sound just like your Brother!

James here sounds like Matthew 5:33–37. It's not exact, but he restates Jesus. Read James 5:12 and then read Matthew 5:33–37:

> [33] Again, you have heard that it was said to the people long ago, 'Do not break your oath, but fulfill to the Lord the vows you have made.' [34] But I tell you, do not swear an oath at all: either by heaven, for it is God's throne; [35] or by the earth, for it is his footstool; or by Jerusalem, for it is the city of the Great King. [36] And do not swear by your head, for you cannot make even one hair white or black. [37] All you need to say is simply 'Yes' or 'No'; anything beyond this comes from the evil one.

What I notice here is that both Jesus and James disagree with the common habit of oath-taking because for Jesus (and for James) oath-taking masks a reality they want to transcend. We take oaths in court because humans often lie and deceive. Jesus wants his followers to embrace a kingdom kind of reality, and that means transparent honesty. So Jesus said, "We don't need oaths because when we are asked, we tell the truth." The Old Testament's permission to use oaths becomes with Jesus the end of a permission. In this Jesus and James are like the Essenes at Qumran, who also prohibited oath-taking. Josephus, who knew the community personally, said, "they say, that he who cannot be believed without [swearing by] God, is already condemned" and that they consider oath-making "worse than perjury."

But is this a law with Jesus and James? A law that is absolutely prohibited? The early Christians evidently didn't follow this as an absolute (Rom. 1:9; Heb. 6:13–20; Rev. 10:6). So we might be wisest to think of this statement, not as a rigid law, but as a warning about the human tendency to deceive and the importance of telling the truth. There is no reason for followers of Jesus to ramp up their honesty quotient with oath-making terms like "by heaven or by earth or by anything else" (James 5:12). When asked, say "Yes" or say "No."

Churches today need to learn from this. When abused people have made allegations against churches—or any institution for that matter—too many leaders and boards and executive committees roll out publicity-conscious press releases instead of simply telling the truth; they discredit the critics, demonize the critics, gaslight the critics, silence the critics, and suppress the critics. The result is that the organizations spin the story around themselves, and spinning a story is not the way of the "Yes" and "No" of Jesus or James.

Christians need to pray. Different conditions shape what we say to God. Troubles lead to prayer, happiness leads to praise, and sicknesses lead to petitions (5:13–14). The ears of the empathic Christian hear what many don't have the ear for. The empathic hear needs, sometimes expressed in groans and other times in the safety of a hint. Good pastors have ears for hints and before long are in the home or at the bedside or simply ready to listen to those in need. James speaks to those in need of healing.

Petitions in the Bible manifest, if one collects them all into a bundle, a pattern for how to ask God for what one wants. The later church tradition of petitionary prayer called "collects" follows this pattern in such a crisp manner that many of us have learned to ask God for something without knowing we have been taught how to do so (McKnight). Those prayers begin by addressing God (Father, Lord Almighty), then turn to a description of God (You are the great healer) that provides the foundation for what one asks. That is, if God is the healer in ages past, then I have every right to ask God to heal me now. So, the address and description are followed by the petition itself (heal me, heal her, heal us) and to this petition is often attached a commitment that implicates the one praying into a life of obedience (so that I may walk in your ways and glorify you). All prayers end, and the Christian prayer tradition ends by praying "in Christ's name" or "through Christ" and uttering the word "Amen."

In his words about petitions, James meanders into a theological exploration. Petitions for healing require faith (5:15) and, because sickness is connected to sin, forgiveness emerges in the same verse, but this prompts the thought of the need to confess sins to one another as a context for petitions for healing (5:16). Confession and forgiveness clean the slate, and the prayer of righteous persons can be effective, which prompts James to think of the great prayer warrior Elijah (5:16–18). He meanders but covers the topic.

James offers his wisdom for how petitions for healing are to be done. *First:* James urges them to call "the elders of the church," who fit the need for a "righteous person." In the apostle Paul's churches they may have asked someone with the "gift of healing" to come to the home (1 Cor. 12:28). *Second:* Petitions for healing were accompanied by anointing, the smearing of olive oil on a person. People anointed wounds and the sick with oil, sometimes hot oils, so this can be taken as medicinal. But more commonly oil consecrated and purified a body as an act of devoting it to God for healing. *Third:* All of this was to be done "in the name of the Lord" because healing was God's act, not the elders'. *Fourth:* Acts like these, when done in prayers of faith, "will make the sick person well," James tells us. To think following this procedure step by step will always yield a healing turns the process into magic. Further, it fails to see healing as God's restorative work and the summons to faith—that is, to trust God to do what God wants. His wisdom for prayers for healing are short and brief, so ours must be too!

Christians need to restore the wandering. No letter ends on a more heartfelt note than James. He grieves over the wandering (from the faith) and, without using an imperative to tell someone to bring them back, he all but does that with a positive reminder of what such a bringing-back accomplishes: it "will save them from death" and it will "cover over a multitude of sins." There is some trendiness in the "deconstruction" many are walking through today, but behind it all are some very, very serious questions. Many are in *angst* about their faith and about the church. They want a way forward. James offers one solid approach: pastoral empathy and care and presence.

We don't know why the person left the faith in James' community. In our day people are walking from the faith because the church has failed to look like Jesus. It lacks compassion, it lacks empathy, and it lacks a commitment to justice and peace. Alongside these concerns one will also find the conflict of science and faith and the literalistic way many read the Bible. These also aggravate the faith of many. Others are offended by raw and heartless teachings about hell and about some passages about God's approval of violence (McKnight and Ondrey). But it is pastorally wise to watch James in this passage: his counsel is not destructive denunciation or heartless dismissals but pastoral empathy and care

Those who restore such persons back to faith cover a mountain of sins, an expression from Proverbs 10:12 and used also by Peter (1 Peter 4:8). Sins are here quantified, and the restorer diminishes their number because the one who returns ceases from such sins. The letter ends abruptly, but we need to remember that the person who delivered the letter and read the letter to the exiled Christians no doubt gave special words to them from James as the reader would also have answered questions that arose in the reading. All this was common for ancient letter writers and readers.

QUESTIONS FOR REFLECTION AND APPLICATION

1. Reflect back on these lessons from the book of James. What most stands out to you? How has this study shaped your view of James' letter?

2. What do you think about the fact that James sounds like his brother Jesus? Can you think of other places James seems to reference words of Jesus?

3. What three separable instructions does James the pastor give the people in his churches?

4. Does your yes mean yes and your no mean no? What do you need to change in your speech habits in order to be a truth-teller?

5. Write a prayer in the style of a collect. Petition God to help you apply the wisdom you have learned from James.

FOR FURTHER READING

Josephus, *Jewish War* 2.135 (Loeb Classical Library).

Scot McKnight, *To You All Hearts Are Open: Revitalizing the Church's Pattern of Asking God* (Brewster, MA: Paraclete, 2021).

Scot McKnight and Hauna Ondrey, *Finding Faith, Losing Faith: Stories of Conversion and Apostasy* (Waco, TX: Baylor University Press, 2008), 7–64.

GALATIANS

INTRODUCTION: READING PAUL'S LETTER TO THE GALATIANS

Some date Galatians at about the same time as Romans, which makes Galatians a bit of an anthology of Romans, while others date Galatians some eight years or so earlier. I'm with the second group, and this means Galatians is Paul's first letter as he attempts to solve a major issue in his mission churches: Judean[1] converts to Jesus as the Messiah expected gentile converts to Jesus to embrace the law of Moses. The letter to the Galatians is Paul's vehement disagreement with those Judean converts, whom I will call his "critics." This heated letter explains an entirely different way to read the Bible now that the Messiah has come and sent the Holy Spirit. For Paul, the arrival of Jesus and the gift of the Spirit unleashed the era of liberation.

---

1. "Judean" means one from Judea or the tribe of Judah, a region of the land of Israel. Jesus was not a Judean but a Galilean. "Jew" anglicizes the term and disrespects the geographical origins. I have mostly used Judean but sometimes Jewish.

The Galatians are in today's central Turkey, near modern Ankara, and the churches were formed in Paul's first missionary journey, so if you look at a map you can see places like Pisidian Antioch, Iconium, Lystra, Derbe—and those are the cities near Galatia.

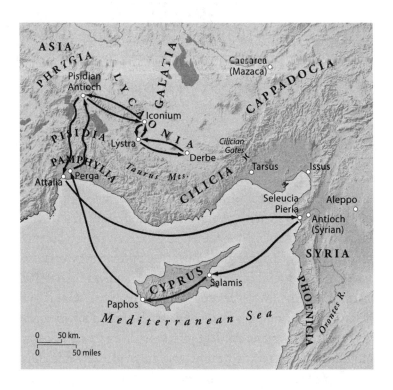

Jerusalem was in a turmoil over Paul's mission churches and those gentile converts who sat loose with respect to the law of Moses. The leading Christian in Jerusalem was the brother of Jesus, James. He was more committed to the law of Moses than Paul. Some people either representing him, or claiming to represent him, arrived in Galatia with the message that fully devoted gentile followers of Jesus are to embrace the law of Moses. Paul responds emotionally, and Galatians deposits for us his sharp disagreements with his critics. The disagreements are at least in part examples of clashing cultures and can't be explained simply as theological differences. Theology works itself into our very bones and behaviors. Differences in theology then are at times differences in what is in our bones and not just what is in our brains. Samuel Jayakumar, in his essay on "Caste" in the *South Asia Bible Commentary*, illustrates both the cultural dimension of Paul's message while also pointing to the redemptive power of inclusion as equals in the church—with persecutions and other exclusions (!) and manifestations of caste in the church. Like Romans 14–15, Galatians exhibits two groups claiming power and privilege: Jewish believers claiming election privilege and the power of the Bible's story while Paul, and those on his side, claimed the liberating gospel and the power of a different way of reading the Bible.

Here is the crux of Paul's argument: Read the Bible starting with Abraham, that is, read Genesis 12 and Genesis 15 if you want to know God's plan. The blessing of Abraham would extend to the gentiles, which is Paul's mission, on the basis of a faith response just like Abraham's faith. Circumcision, which embodies what Paul means by the "works of the law," is not how Abraham experienced the blessing. Gentiles and Judeans enter into the family of Abraham by faith, not by observing the law of Moses. Paul explains all this and far more in Galatians 3:15–25, and the passage is so important to understand that we begin this *Everyday Bible Study* there. The message of these verses determines why they all need to be unified and why the leading term for the Christian community is "liberty" or "freedom." So, I would not blame you if you chose then to read the study on Galatians 2:11–21, where we see unity fractured, and then the theme verse about liberation at Galatians 5:1—and only then went back to Galatians 1:1. But at least we have to get the big picture in mind and that comes by thinking our way through 3:15–25.

One formula expresses the heart of the message of this letter:

CHRIST IS ENOUGH.

Addition to Christ subtracts Christ. That is, subtraction by addition.

Whatever one thinks needs to be added—one's special theology, one's special experiences, one's denomination, one's special pastor—will result in questioning the adequacy of Christ.

"Christ is enough" then is the formula.

Easier to declare than to live. That's why we have Galatians. Let's dive in.

FOR FURTHER STUDY

Shaye J. D. Cohen, study notes to Galatians in *The Jewish Annotated New Testament* (New York: Oxford University Press, 2011), 332–344.
David deSilva, *Galatians*, New International

Commentary on the New Testament (Grand Rapids: Wm. B. Eerdmans, 2018).

James D. G. Dunn, *The Epistle to the Galatians*, Black's New Testament Commentaries (Peabody, MA: Hendrickson, 1993).

Samuel Jayakumar, "Caste," *South Asia Bible Commentary*, 1622–1623.

Scot McKnight, *Galatians*, NIV Application Commentary (Grand Rapids: Zondervan, 1995).

N. T. Wright, *Galatians*, Commentaries for Christian Formation (Grand Rapids: Wm. B. Eerdmans, 2021).

Dating Paul's Life

Early Period: Who's in the Church? (48–57)

Galatians (48)

What Are the Problems?:

1–2 Thessalonians (50)

1, 2 Corinthians (54, 56)

Romans (57)

Prison Ministry: What Is the Church? (53–55?)

Philemon, Colossians, Philippians (c. 53, 54, 55 or 63?)

Ephesians (c. 55)

Later Period: What Will the Church Be? (60–62, perhaps 64)

1–2 Timothy, Titus (c. early 60s)

CHRIST IS ENOUGH!

Galatians 3:15–25

Special Note to the Reader: You may ask why our first passage is from the middle of the book and not the letter's beginning. And why begin with the most complicated passage in the whole letter to the Galatians at that! There's a good reason: nothing makes sense in Paul's letter to the Galatians (modern-day Turkey, near Ankara) until the basic ideas found in Galatians 3:15–25 become instincts. This passage explains in short, quick statements how Paul reads the Bible.

> [15] *Brothers and sisters, let me take an example from every-day life. Just as no one can set aside or add to a human covenant that has been duly established, so it is in this case.* [16] *The promises were spoken to Abraham and to his seed. Scripture does not say "and to seeds," meaning many people, but "and to your seed," meaning one person, who is Christ.* [17] *What I mean is this: The law, introduced 430 years later, does not set aside the covenant previously established by God and thus do away with the promise.* [18] *For if the inheritance depends on the law, then it no longer depends on the promise; but God in his grace gave it to Abraham through a promise.*

[19]Why, then, was the law given at all? It was added because of transgressions until the Seed to whom the promise referred had come. The law was given through angels and entrusted to a mediator. [20]A mediator, however, implies more than one party; but God is one.

[21]Is the law, therefore, opposed to the promises of God? Absolutely not! For if a law had been given that could impart life, then righteousness would certainly have come by the law. [22]But Scripture has locked up everything under the control of sin, so that what was promised, being given through faith in Jesus Christ, might be given to those who believe.

[23]Before the coming of this faith, we were held in custody under the law, locked up until the faith that was to come would be revealed. [24]So the law was our guardian until Christ came that we might be justified by faith. [25]Now that this faith has come, we are no longer under a guardian.

Paul can get very complicated. The apostle Peter said the same thing. So here's the big picture before we get into Paul's (important) complications:

- **Paul's critics:** "Serious followers of Jesus must observe the law of Moses. It's right here in our Bible."
- **Paul:** "All followers of Jesus have been liberated from the law. It's a new world."

Everywhere Paul went, his critics seemed to follow. We are lucky Paul wrote Galatians (and then later Romans) to explain it all. It gets complicated, but keep those lines above in mind, and it will help.

Again, we are beginning this Study with the most complicated passage in the whole letter to the Galatians. This passage explains in short, quick statements how Paul reads the Bible. When the Galatians listened to someone read this letter to them, some in the room were cheering him on while others were grumbling aloud and mumbling to one another. Some had heard this stuff before, but others were hearing it for the first time in Paul's own words.

The heart of his argument is in this passage, and Paul assumed the basics of this passage for every line in this letter. Once we finish this passage and move on to the opening of the letter, you'll agree. Or at least I hope you'll agree.

Some Judean[1] believers in Galatia grew up on the Torah (law) of Moses and knew that circumcision was God's requirement for all males under the covenant, including converts to Judaism. Their Bible taught converts to observe the whole law. So, when gentiles were converting to faith in Jesus as the Messiah of Israel, it was altogether natural for the Judean believers to expect gentiles to become full converts to Israel's now-complete faith. Anyone reading the first five books of the Bible, and especially anyone who was nurtured in the kind of Judean faith they were nurtured in, would expect gentile converts to observe the law. But Paul's way of reading the Bible surprised them all. The Judean believers considered him mistaken and many in Jerusalem agreed. Just read Acts 21–23. His critics in Galatia were emissaries of his critics in Jerusalem.

---

1. The Greek word *youdaios* is behind our translations. It means "Judean," one from Judea or the tribe of Judah, a region of the Land of Israel. Jesus was not a Judean but a Galilean. "Jew" anglicizes the term and disrespects the geographical origins. I have mostly used Judean but sometimes Jewish.

Paul's ideas form into a timeline of three eras and into seven history-altering claims. Yes, history-altering because Paul's reading of the Bible was at odds with his critics in Galatia. If you keep your eyes on the timeline it will make sense. Think of it this way. Some grew up, as I did, with a manual typewriter, and we went through its improvements, whether an electric typewriter or an IBM Selectric. They were all still typewriters. We fed it paper and snapped in a ribbon or cartridge. When we typed the wrong letter, we had to cover our mistakes with white "liquid paper" or a clever little piece of tape that removed the letters. Then came the computer era, and when the computer arrived, we—at least most of us—put away our typewriters and learned how to live in a new era. So with Paul: the Era of law is a typewriter age, and we are in the age of the computer, which is the Era of Christ. Paul says typing on a typewriter in the age of a computer is to fall back from the grace and faith and justification of the Era of Christ. (Do you know what it's like to write a book on a manual typewriter?)

There are three eras for Paul: the Promise Era, the Law Era, and the Christ Era. We can call these Anticipation, Slavery, and Liberation.

His critics wanted to live in both the Christ Era and the Law Era, and Paul said one had to choose. Nearly every line in this letter is about some Judean believers wanting gentile believers to be "fully devoted" in following Christ by observing the law of Moses. Every line in the letter is about learning to leave the Era of Moses and live in the Era of Christ. Not all of these terms are found in Galatians 3:15–25, but they are present in Galatians itself.

THREE ERAS IN THE STORY OF ISRAEL

PROMISE (430 years)	LAW ⇨	CHRIST
God		God
Abraham (transgressions)	Angels (sin)	
	Moses	
Covenant Promise	Law (until)	Gospel
	Guardians	Fruit of the Spirit
Grace		Grace
	Flesh	Spirit
Inheritance		Inheritance
		God as Father
		Adoption/Family
Faith	Works of the law	Faith
Justification	Curse	Justification
Righteousness		Righteousness
Blessing		Blessing
Life	Death	Life
ANTICIPATION	SLAVERY	LIBERATION

Paul has one goal, and it goes all capital letters in Galatians 5:1: LIBERATION. We are now liberated in Christ, liberated from the law, liberated from sin, liberated from slavery, liberated from the flesh, liberated from death, liberated in the Spirit, liberated for the fruit of the Spirit, liberated for life, and liberated for what God made us to be! We need to know our Era, and we need to live in that Era. We need to stay in our lane. A life of liberation is found only in the Era of Christ. If we are liberated in Christ, then the gentile believers do not have to follow the law of Moses. If the law of Moses brings life, we don't need Christ. Make your choice. Choose your column.

Paul loved to read the Bible with precision—after all, he grew up a Pharisee. They were the ones known as the Bible specialists. But his precision is not like some theological sophistications today. Believe me, I've heard plenty of them. After listening to a long explanation about something, you may blurt out, "So what!" and be right in your blurting. Not so with Paul. Each of Paul's seven, somewhat complicated, points matters as a cumulative case. We have to pay careful attention because his case matters to us. Every Christian group, just like Paul's critics in Galatia, finds ways to squash freedom in Christ by adding something to "Christ is enough." If your church doesn't, it's the first one in almost 2,000 years!

Now to the seven history-altering claims. Read them through slowly a couple of times before you read my brief explanations. You'll be surprised, first, at Paul's brilliant logic that all leads to "Christ is enough" and, second, at the radical change these seven points bring to reading the Bible in a new way (at least for his critics in Galatia). Beth and Melissa Moore say this so well: "What I'm starting to get my head around—even be compelled by—is that Paul was, in some revolutionary ways, already living in a new world" (*Faith Has Come*, 105).

1. Everything starts with the Promise (not the law of Moses).
2. The law was added later, had a limited purpose, and was for a limited time.
3. The law is inferior to the promise.
4. The law cannot bring life.
5. The proper response is promise-era faith, not Moses-era "works of the law."
6. The time for the law-as-guardian is over.
7. The aim in history all along was Christ.
   ⇨ Christ is enough. No additions!
      ⇨ Therefore, we are liberated.

Brief explanations now of each.

#1: Everything starts with the Promise. The simplicity of the point masks the profundity of its implications. God gave a covenant-promise to Abram/Abraham (Genesis 12; 15). In law, if you have a covenant formed and you add some codicil (supplementary document), the codicil does not undermine the covenant (Galatians 3:15–18). So with Abraham and Moses. Moses' does not alter Abraham's covenant promise. The fundamental agreement God makes with Israel is the Promise, not the Law; Abraham, not Moses. This is radical, friends, because for Paul's critics, Moses was Abraham 2.0. That is, the Moses Era updated and replaced the Abraham Era. But

Paul reads the Bible another way: the basic, unalterable agreement is with Abraham in the form of a covenant promise. Which raises the Question of Questions among the Galatians. If Abraham's promise is all that is needed, "Why then the law?" Paul has just said the Promise matters more than the law, and his critics must have thought Paul had denied the Bible. Why, then, even give the law? Two answers are given.

> A covenant is a mutual agreement between two parties that involves promise (blessings) and requirements for both sides. The covenant God makes with Abraham/Israel makes Israel part of God's family with the requirement to live faithfully before God (Sandra Richter). It is notable that Paul sees the covenant in terms of its promise to bless the nations through Israel (Christopher Wright).

#2 The law was added later, had a limited purpose, and was for a limited time period. God forms a covenant promise with Abraham, but covenant people, it was easy to see, were transgressing God's ways, so God adds the law to unmask transgressions as sin (Rom. 3:20; 5:20; 7:7). That's the purpose of the law. Along with this limited purpose, the law was also only for a limited time. It was given "until the Seed to whom the promise referred had come." Until Jesus. These two points of Paul's cut into the entire program of those who believed gentiles would need to embrace the whole law if they wanted to be in good standing in the covenant people. No, Paul says, the Era of the Law ends at the Era of Christ.

#3: The law is inferior to the promise. Paul moves now to "let's talk among ourselves" argument: the promise was given *directly* from God to Abraham, but the law was given through *mediation*. God gave it to angels who gave it to Moses (see Acts 7:38, 43; Hebrews 2:2). Therefore, the promise is superior to the law since it involved no mediation. Paul's friends in Galatia—especially the men now realizing they would not need the entry card called circumcision—were clapping, but his critics were not impressed. They feared the implications of this radical view of Paul. This point led to another question. If the law is inferior to the promise, is the law against the promises? Paul unequivocally says "No!" and whoever read this letter would have at this point slowed down and said it clearly. With a long pause following. Lots of harumphing would have been heard. They're thinking "this sounds a little too loose and liberating for us."

Because **#4: The law cannot bring life. Only the promise brings life.** Paul insinuates that his critics think promise + law brings life. We read that very view in the later Judean collection called the *Mishnah*: "lots of Torah, lots of life" (*m. Abot* 2:8). That is, for them there is no promise without law, no covenant without law, no people of God without the law. Paul says, No, read the Bible all over again as if for the first time. The promise, not the law, brings life. Everything begins with that covenant promise with Abraham. He digs in his heels with this: the law actually imprisoned humans in sin. The law was designed to be "our guardian until Christ came." Limited purpose (to reveal sin) for a limited time (from Moses to Christ).

In the diagram shown earlier, you can see that the Era of Abraham matches the Era of Christ. Both involve grace, faith, life, inheritance, and justification. The Era of Moses brings law and consciousness of sin and slavery and imprisonment and death. Moses did his job, and it is now the Era of Christ, so the gentile believers do not have to observe the law of Moses. They are liberated.

Let's remind ourselves again where Paul is headed: Christ is enough! No additions needed.

#5: The response that unleashes life is faith, not "works of the law." Since life comes through promise and the response to promise was faith, life comes to us by way of faith. Life here means being "justified," or being made right with God. Justification is by faith in Christ, not by works of the law. Again, Christ is enough.

#6: So, the time for the law-as-guardian is over. We can all guess that the words of Galatians 3:25 did not go over well with at least some of his vocal critics in Galatia: "Now that this faith has come, we are no longer under a guardian." That means the limited time is up and the limited purpose is over, and it is now time to live in the Era of Christ through the power of the Spirit. Paul describes the time from Moses to Christ as a time of Israel being but a child, but with Christ, adulting comes. One more time, Christ is enough and has liberated us from the works of the law.

#7: The aim of the promise all along was Jesus. There is a very subtle word Paul decides to exploit in a very Judean manner in Galatians 3:16: Paul turns the word "seed" in Genesis (12:7; 13:15; 24:7), which is a collective singular, into a simple singular and claims the promise all along was spoken to Christ. Just read again Galatians 3:19; 3:22; and 3:23–25. So, this last claim can be called the first claim. When one sees what happens to the Story of Israel in Christ, one has a completely different reading of that Story.

That is the very essence of Paul's problem with the Galatians: they needed a new lesson in how to read the Bible. What they needed to do was to realize that the coming of Christ revolutionized their Story and how best to read the Bible.

Everything in Galatians is based on the timeline above or, put differently, on this revolutionary reading of the Bible. The implication for us today is this: since Christ is enough, we have been liberated from the law and from any additions to Christ. We need to avoid adding anything to Christ, being judged by additions and judging others by our favorite additions. Christ is enough. We are liberated in Christ. We are tempted in our day to judge people by their race, by their ethnicity, by their politics, by their education, by their wealth, by their gender, by their clothing, by their status, and by their appearance. All these divide us into groups. These dividing lines turn us into competitors, into warriors, and at times even into enemies. "One hundred times no!" Paul says. By Christ and in Christ, all these have been dismantled as status symbols and as judgments. If Christ is enough, we are all enough in Christ!

That's liberation.

QUESTIONS FOR REFLECTION AND APPLICATION

1. Why does McKnight begin this examination of Galatians in 3:15–25 instead of in chapter 1?

2. What does McKnight say is Paul's one goal in one word? Do you agree that this sums up Paul's view? Why or why not?

3. What are the three Eras for Paul that McKnight offers? What are the alternate names he gives for each Era?

4. Look at the seven history-altering claims. Which one challenges your current view of Galatians and Paul most, and why?

5. If Christ is truly enough, what does that change for your life and the way you live your faith?

FOR FURTHER READING

David deSilva, *Galatians*, New International Commentary on the New Testament (Grand Rapids: Wm. B. Eerdmans, 2018).

John Goldingay, *Israel's Gospel*, Old Testament Theology Series, vol. 1 (Downers Grove, IL: IVP Academic, 2015), 193–287.

Beth and Melissa Moore, *Faith Has Come* (Houston: Living Proof Ministries, 2020).

Sandra Richter, *The Epic of Eden* (Grand Rapids: HarperChristian Resources, 2021), 69–91.

Christopher J. H. Wright, *The Mission of God* (Downers Grove, IL: IVP Academic, 2018), 191–221.

SURPRISES FOR THE GOSPEL OF LIBERATION

Galatians 1:1–10

[1] Paul, an apostle—sent not from men nor by a man, but by Jesus Christ and God the Father, who raised him from the dead—[2] and all the brothers and sisters with me,

To the churches in Galatia:

[3] Grace and peace to you from God our Father and the Lord Jesus Christ, [4] who gave himself for our sins to rescue us from the present evil age, according to the will of our God and Father, [5] to whom be glory for ever and ever. Amen.

[6] I am astonished that you are so quickly deserting the one who called you to live in the grace of Christ and are turning to a different gospel—[7] which is really no gospel at all. Evidently some people are throwing you into confusion and are trying to pervert the gospel of Christ. [8] But even if we or an angel from heaven should preach a gospel other than the one we preached to you, let them be under God's curse! [9] As we have already said, so now I say again: If anybody is preaching to you a gospel other than what you accepted, let them be under God's curse!

> [10] *Am I now trying to win the approval of human beings,*
> *or of God? Or am I trying to please people? If I were still*
> *trying to please people, I would not be a servant of Christ.*

The gospel matters. The stakes are high. If you don't pull weeds from your garden, they take over; if you text when you drive, you endanger your life and the lives of others; if you eat an unhealthy diet and avoid exercise, you put your health in jeopardy; if you don't visit the dentist regularly, you may ruin your teeth . . . we could add others. Your health matters, your vegetables matter, your life matters. The gospel matters. If you corrupt the gospel, you corrupt redemption. The stakes are high. How do we corrupt the gospel today? Let's get this on the table right away:

- When we add status to the gospel
- When we add wealth to the gospel
- When we add marriage to the gospel
- When we add education to the gospel
- When we add our pastor to the gospel
- When we add a translation to the gospel
- When we add partisan politics to the gospel
- When we add denominational theology to the gospel
- When we add hot button in-the-news-all-day to the gospel

Adding these to the gospel corrupts the gospel. That is, when we decide certain persons are not acceptable to us and to God. That is, when we decide that we decide who is "in" and who is "out," we have added to the gospel. We can point at the critics of Paul all we want, but we are better off realizing what they were doing is as common as bubbles on soap. Christ is enough, and *his enough needs to be our enough.*

It seems so clear, so simple, so easy.

Only it's not.

Surprises pop up constantly for those who are liberated.

SURPRISING HIS CRITICS

The growth of the gospel in the mission of Paul *surprised* the Judeans, whether they believed in Jesus as Messiah or not. No doubt some of the growth surprised Paul himself. His critics were surprised, too. They were proud of the gentile believers who did choose to embrace the observance of the law of Moses, but they were surprised—stunned might be a better word—when Paul stepped in and enforced a Time Out so he could straighten things out. Just skip over a page or two in your Bible to Galatians 2:11–14 and read about the explosive situation with Peter and Barnabas and the guys with the tool designed for circumcision. Such an incident exposes the surprising tensions in Galatia.

This letter gets going faster than any of Paul's letters. Unlike his other letters, he doesn't even express thanks for the Galatians. But his emotional energy to get on with it doesn't prevent Paul from a few customary niceties of letters. He identifies himself and defines his apostleship: "sent not from men nor by a man, but by Jesus Christ and God the Father." It's subtle, but his critics in Galatia were already on their heels. He *surprised* them in the first sentence. He claims that he doesn't need their approval because God commissioned him to the gospel work he's doing. We'll see this more than once in the first two chapters. He's not the only one behind this letter as it comes also from other siblings in Christ who are with him.

His greeting is both common to the Greek world ("grace") and the Judean world ("peace"). These two words are magical in Paul's own special lexicon. He links them to redemption in 1:4 ("who gave himself . . ."). Believers are in view. "Our sins" and "rescue us" and "our God" show this. You might be *surprised* how Paul says this, though. He doesn't say we are "forgiven" of our sins, but we are "rescued"—this is exodus language—from a time period, and this time period is both the Era of Moses and the "present evil age." In the Judean world of Paul, there were two ages, the present age and the age to come (Matt. 12:32). Paul works with that idea, but for him the Era of Moses belongs to the present age that is passing away or perishing (1 Cor. 2:6; Eph. 5:16). Christ lifts them out of one Era to relocate them in the Christ Era. Redemption is time zone change. These believers move from slavery to the law of Moses into the liberation of Christ.

The gospel matters. It matters ultimately.

SURPRISING PAUL

Which is why Paul is himself so *surprised*. His own words are, "I am astonished"—stunned, shocked, bewildered, utterly dumbfounded. The gentile believers who have entered the transfer portal to another team—the Judean team that believes true believers must also fully embrace the law of Moses—shock Paul. He takes their sudden shift all the way to the bottom. They have abandoned "the one who called you to live in the grace of Christ" and shifted "to a different gospel." Put scare quotes around "gospel" there. This gospel, he now says, "is really no gospel"! To move back in time from the Era of Christ and liberation to the Era of Moses and slavery to the law is to abandon the gospel. Those who add to the gospel subtract the gospel from the equation. Think about that a little bit. Adding anything to the gospel deconstructs the gospel. One can't live in two eras. One either lives in the Era of Moses or the Era of Christ.

His critics are causing confusion and actually perverting the gospel. Paul doubles down on this one because the gospel is at stake.

What is the gospel for Paul? Paul defines it in 1 Corinthians 15:3–5 in a way that makes clear he did not define the gospel but those who were before him did:

> that Christ died for our sins according to the Scriptures,
> that he was buried,
> that he was raised on the third day according to the
>   Scriptures,
> and that he appeared to Cephas, and then to the Twelve.

The gospel is the story about Jesus "according to the Scriptures," that is, the story of Christ that fulfills the Story of Israel (McKnight). Paul reduces this even more in 2 Timothy 2:8 when he summarizes the gospel as "remember Jesus Christ, raised from the dead, descended from David" and he adds, "This is my gospel." The gospel is the story about Jesus that rescues people on the basis of God's grace. The response to this gospel is faith—faith forming into faithfulness or allegiance (Bates)—and not observance of the law of Moses ("works of the law" in Gal. 2:16). Paul is a radical: the gospel, which fulfills the Promise given to Abraham, is the entire foundation to his theology and to his practice. A lived theology of the gospel means Jesus is enough, the Spirit is our power, grace is God's gift to us, and we are to live in trusting allegiance. Anything that corrupts these points destroys the gospel.

Okay, you may ask, what's the point? The critics of Paul asserted the necessity of observing the law, and Paul knows that observing the law undercuts the shift from the Era of Moses to the Era of Christ. In the Era of Christ, there is liberation from the law. To shift from Christ to Moses erases the gospel of the new era. It *surprises* Paul that anyone, to borrow from the previous chapter, would move back to a typewriter when they have a computer.

Paul ramps up language in a way we will not see again in all his letters. This too is a *surprise*. Those who announce a gospel that combines Moses with Christ, those who declare a gospel anything other than the gospel about Jesus he previously preached to them are "under God's curse" (Gal. 1:8, 9). The term he uses entails a double sense: first, handing the false-gospel preacher over to God and, second, for the purpose of utter destruction. Similar fierce words are found in Leviticus 27:29: "No person devoted to destruction may be ransomed; they are to be put to death." Paul is not taking matters into his own hands here. He's not becoming a medieval Crusader. No, he's handing this person over to God for God to do what God does.

SURPRISING US TODAY

What *surprises* me is what comes next. Evidently, some critics were putting up graffiti on the synagogue walls of Galatia saying that Paul was a people-pleaser. Remember, he made it clear in 1:1 that his gospel is not by humans or from humans. So, perhaps what we read in Galatians 1:10 explains even more why he wrote what he did in 1:1. Evidently, at one time he was seeking approval from humans, which Paul admits when he says "still" in 1:10. He's referring to his pre-conversion days when he was seeking approval from religious, rabbinic authorities in Jerusalem. But he was converted (1:11–24). He shifted from the Era of Moses where his approval came from those who mediated the law to him. He turned from them to Christ and became the slave (better than "servant" in the NIV) of Christ. He wants them to know that he seeks only the approval of God as Christ's slave. His critics must have thought he had reduced gospel demands—no observance of the law of Moses—so he could gain more converts. So they think he's a people-pleaser instead of a God-pleaser, which for them would mean a higher level of commitment. Every item I listed at the beginning of this passage that is added to the gospel is taken by someone as this higher level of commitment. But, no, adding to the gospel eradicates it.

No longer is he a people-pleaser. Pause a moment to ponder how often we are motivated by pleasing someone, how often what others will say reshapes what we want thought of us, and how often we exercise our power to get people to please us. Paul has put pleasing people, the people who populate the Moses Era, behind him. He now lives in the Era of Christ, the era of liberation. The gospel matters. Life in the new era brings surprises at every turn because the stakes are so high.

We need to have some sympathy for all these surprises. Living with "Christ is enough" is not easy. We love to add to the gospel; we love to add our preferences and our privileges and our power to the gospel. The stripping away of preferences, privileges, and power is painful. If Christ is enough, we need to tear down all additions to Christ and learn to live with *Christ is enough*. It's the way of liberation.

QUESTIONS FOR REFLECTION AND APPLICATION

1. Explain how adding to the gospel distorts the gospel.

2. How does Paul define the gospel?

3. Who are the three people or groups of people this passage surprises? How is each surprised by these words?

4. How does Paul's conversion impact his previous people-pleasing problem? How could a better understanding of the gospel help prevent your people-pleasing?

5. Get honest with yourself and consider, "What have I added to the gospel?"

FOR FURTHER READING

Matthew W. Bates, *Gospel Allegiance* (Grand Rapids: Brazos, 2019).

Scot McKnight, *The King Jesus Gospel* (Grand Rapids: Zondervan, 2011).

CONTESTING
LIBERATION

Galatians 1:11–24

[11] I want you to know, brothers and sisters, that the gospel I preached is not of human origin. [12] I did not receive it from any man, nor was I taught it; rather, I received it by revelation from Jesus Christ.

[13] For you have heard of my previous way of life in Judaism, how intensely I persecuted the church of God and tried to destroy it. [14] I was advancing in Judaism beyond many of my own age among my people and was extremely zealous for the traditions of my fathers. [15] But when God, who set me apart from my mother's womb and called me by his grace, was pleased [16] to reveal his Son in me so that I might preach him among the Gentiles, my immediate response was not to consult any human being. [17] I did not go up to Jerusalem to see those who were apostles before I was, but I went into Arabia. Later I returned to Damascus.

[18] Then after three years, I went up to Jerusalem to get acquainted with Cephas and stayed with him fifteen days. [19] I saw none of the other apostles—only James, the Lord's

brother. ²⁰ I assure you before God that what I am writing you is no lie.

²¹ Then I went to Syria and Cilicia. ²² I was personally unknown to the churches of Judea that are in Christ. ²³ They only heard the report: "The man who formerly persecuted us is now preaching the faith he once tried to destroy." ²⁴ And they praised God because of me.

R This happens today, but not so often with white men. Women and people of color are often not respected for the calling they sense is from God. Or they indirectly hear, "Yes, you may be called. Just not here," when *here* means "in our privileged white spaces." Or they are tokenized in such spaces and hear, "We've invited a black man to preach today," when last week's guest speaker had a name. God knows whom God has called even when some are asking, "Where did this person get the idea she was called?"

Paul was asked the same thing. Paul's letters, it has often been said accurately, are like listening to one end of a phone conversation. Or in our terms, it's like reading a tweet and wondering what it's responding to. (Scratch an exclamation point in the margin if you've had this happen.) Some people pushed back against Paul's claims for a liberated life with questions like these: "Who taught you this, Paul? This is not what we learned in synagogue. We know there are many rabbis, but which rabbi taught you this? Is your theory about liberation from the Bible?"

His answer pulled the curtain back but fast. His answer, which extends from 1:11 all the way through the end of chapter two—and some would say through chapter four—reveals more about Paul's own life than any of Paul's letters, so this is a bit of a treat for us. (Ancient writers were not so consumed with their own story as we are today.)

Perhaps a word of consolation: many assume that if we are on truth's side, since truth is compelling (at least to us), others will agree. Nothing could be further from reality if we watch the life of Paul. Everywhere he went, opponents popped up. Not because he was mean or strident but because his message—gospel for all, gospel without law observance for gentiles—was too much for too many. A radical gospel of "Christ is enough" is uncomfortable for many people in all places at all times. Thinking everyone will agree with the gospel of liberation lands us in the mire of wondering if we are right. Knowing that not everyone will hop in the boat prevents the frustrations of too-high expectations. Our passage reveals the trouble Paul constantly experienced. His claims were often rejected. People contested his source-claim for the liberation gospel.

I Got My Liberation Message from God

In our previous passage the apostle Paul rather abruptly announced that he was not a people-pleaser. Instead, he was pleasing God, and he made the surprising claim that he's had a one-on-one with God. He's saying, "No one told me or gave it to me or taught me. God spoke to me. God told me what to say." His words: "the gospel I preached is not of human origin," or is not consistent with human-derived ideas. He continues to say that he did not get it in the normal rabbinic method of passing things on from one teacher to his students, that is, he was not taught his gospel. The lexicon Paul learned in sitting at the feet of his rabbi, Gamaliel, provided no help for his message. He now says it in plain language: "I received it by revelation from Jesus Christ" (1:12). We can't minimize the impact of his experience of Christ on the road to Damascus. This was nothing short of an absolute revolution in his life (deSilva).

Paul tells his own story as vivid contrasts between who he was and who he is now. First, he states he had high status among other budding rabbis. He speaks of "advancing in Judaism beyond many of my own age among my people." He admits he was "extremely zealous for the traditions of my fathers." He was an A student, fiercely punishing the followers of Jesus, destined to be a rabbi of rabbis (like his teacher Gamaliel), known for his passionate devotion to study, observing every *mitzvah*, mastering the interpretive conclusions of those who were experts in the law of Moses. Then he turned to Jesus. For many Paul was an apostate, but Paul still saw himself as a Jew, as a fulfilled one. The power in Paul's story, too, is tethered to the contrasts between his former and present life.

That contrast with who he *was* mic-drop ends with three words: "But when God" (1:15). Two things explode from these three words. Paul didn't get his ideas about the gospel of liberation from isolation and personal discovery, and he didn't get it from other humans in the rabbi-like fashion. God spoke to him. The most noticeable sign of most conversions is a revision of one's own autobiography

(McKnight). Paul's a convert, not from Judaism to Christianity so much as from the Moses Era to the Jesus Era! Paul now captures his entire life in terms of God's preparation for his calling as an apostle: "who set me apart from my mother's womb." In our terms he could have said, "I was made for this very calling." Like Beth Moore for teaching the Bible, like Fred Rogers for working with children, like Isabel Wilkerson for unmasking racism's structures in the USA, like Eugene Peterson for exploring the spiritual life, like Diane Langberg for exposing power abuse in churches, and like Lynn Cohick for explaining women in the world of the New Testament. He and they were made for that calling.

Paul's message is direct. He got it *from* Jesus (1:12) and it was *about* Jesus: "to reveal his Son"—and here the Greek is not as clear as our translations would like. It could be to reveal his Son *in* me, which sounds a bit like an inner experience, or to reveal his Son *in and through* me, which sounds like his mission. The second option is better because Paul's next words concern his mission. That is, in and through Paul, God was at work "so that," he says, "I might preach him among the Gentiles" (1:16). If you get an open-schedule day and choose to read quickly through Paul's letters in chronological order (see Introduction), you will see from Galatians to Ephesians a clear-cut mission emphasis: his calling, which at times he calls the "mystery," is to preach the gospel to the gentiles and to form churches that combine new gentile with new Judean believers into one new family of God. Yes, they didn't always mix well, and that's why we have both Galatians and Romans. (So, give God some thanks for the troublemakers.)

Here we are then: Paul's claim is that God prepared him for this calling, that God has now revealed his Son to him, and through him God wants this message to go to the entire Roman empire. That liberation message means gentile believers don't have to observe the Torah to be fully devoted followers of Jesus. He got that liberation message from God.

No You Didn't, Paul!

Paul's critics rejected his claims. They had some "what about" questions over his claims of getting this directly from God. They knew Paul had been to Jerusalem. If he had been there, he could have gotten it from someone there. If so, then they wanted to know if those believers in Jerusalem were on board with Paul's liberation message. Did he get it from James (Yakōbos)? Or from Peter (Petros)? Or from the churches now flourishing in Judea?

This gets tricky, so I'll try to explain the complication. His critics wanted damaging information. Since his critics are pretty sure Paul *did not get his radical liberation message from these authorities, then he must be out of sync and on his own and out on a limb, and that would mean he's wrong and this liberation stuff has got to be junked and the law of Moses added to his discipleship program.* They think they are right. Their questions, which we have to reconstruct on the basis of Paul's answers, are accusations of Paul being a liberal innovator. His answers, which emphasize his own independence from Jerusalem's authorities, both play into their hands (yes, this is not based on those authorities) and grabs their satisfactions right back (God gave it to me). One more time now: his critics can't argue that Paul's message is dependent and thus an innovation because Paul admits it is independent of the authorities in Jerusalem. But they also can't argue against him because he says he got it from God! Who wants to argue with God?! They're stuck in a corner with a decision to make. Is the liberation message from God or not?

At times the only confidence some can gain for their calling is inner confidence and certainty that God called. Witheringly relentless criticisms can debilitate that call, but in the nights of prayer and pleadings with God, they hear, as Paul did, the voice of God and remember when they were called. That person realizes, also with Paul, that their critics are not the ones who determine the calling. God does.

YES, I DID!

Paul says in several ways that his message did not come from the authorities in Jerusalem. On the basis of his own words, we could perhaps construct an argument that no matter how much he denies dependence, he was in Jerusalem long enough and with the right people to have learned the true gospel from them. If he did, then he's the one departing from the norm, so they think. Not so according to Paul.

Now quickly—his conversion did not lead him to Jerusalem for affirmation or approval (1:17). He went to Arabia and then to Damascus. It was three years later that he went to Jerusalem to converse with or, better yet, to interview Peter (1:18), and he also met James, brother of Jesus (1:19). The story he is telling of independence, obviously, is not *total* independence. He has in effect put both Peter and James in a corner. The critics can go right to them (and some are from Jerusalem and from James, so they say according to 2:12) and ask if they told Paul he could preach a law-free gospel.

> If they say Yes, they are in the dock.
> If they say No, Paul is in the dock.
> Their case is ready.

He adds to this that he left Jerusalem and went to Syria, then to modern-day Turkey's Cilicia, near his home in Tarsus. The churches around Jerusalem never met him. He's given them a little space, so what does he do?

Paul jabs them with an almost unnoticeable moment. The churches of Judea "praised God because of me" (1:24). He's independent alright because he got his message from God, but he can also say the churches in the area of Jerusalem approved what he was doing. If that's not a backdoor entry into his critics' game, nothing is. And before he's done, he'll add that its principal leaders (James, Cephas, John; 2:9) approved it too! Which is like adding Dallas Willard, the pope, and Tim Keller as endorsements on your book.

Of course, we'd love to know what they said back. We don't know, but this beautiful letter, one end of that conversation, survived. At least they didn't burn it up!

The message of liberation will always be contested.

QUESTIONS FOR REFLECTION
AND APPLICATION

1. Who gave Paul his message and calling? What were they about?

2. Summarize the explanation given here for the line of thought and the strategy of Paul's critics.

3. What comprised Paul's rabbinic training? What were his qualifications as a Judean scholar and teacher?

4. Is the liberation gospel—"the radical gospel of 'Christ is enough'"—an acceptable idea in your church or a foreign one? Does your community have any of its own equivalent expectations to "law observance for gentiles"?

5. Have you ever experienced a questioning of your calling, qualifications, or credentials? Or witnessed that questioning happen to someone else? How did it affect your or their view of calling and ministry work?

FOR FURTHER READING

David deSilva, *Galatians*, New International
  Commentary on the New Testament (Grand Rapids:
  Wm. B. Eerdmans, 2018), 149–156.
Scot McKnight, *Pastor Paul* (Grand Rapids: Brazos, 2019),
  127–144.

EVENTS OF LIBERATION

Galatians 2:1–10

¹ *Then after fourteen years, I went up again to Jerusalem, this time with Barnabas. I took Titus along also.* ² *I went in response to a revelation and, meeting privately with those esteemed as leaders, I presented to them the gospel that I preach among the Gentiles. I wanted to be sure I was not running and had not been running my race in vain.* ³ *Yet not even Titus, who was with me, was compelled to be circumcised, even though he was a Greek.* ⁴ *This matter arose because some false believers had infiltrated our ranks to spy on the liberation we have in Christ Jesus and to make us slaves.* ⁵ *We did not give in to them for a moment, so that the truth of the gospel might be preserved for you.*

⁶ *As for those who were held in high esteem—whatever they were makes no difference to me; God does not show favoritism—they added nothing to my message.* ⁷ *On the contrary, they recognized that I had been entrusted with the task of preaching the gospel to the uncircumcised, just as Peter had been to the circumcised.* ⁸ *For God, who was*

at work in Peter as an apostle to the circumcised, was also at work in me as an apostle to the Gentiles. [9] James, Cephas, and John, those esteemed as pillars, gave me and Barnabas the right hand of fellowship when they recognized the grace given to me. They agreed that we should go to the Gentiles, and they to the circumcised. [10] All they asked was that we should continue to remember the poor, the very thing I had been eager to do all along.

S ometimes an event tells the whole story. Sometimes they are dramatic events. Think of the Selma march led by those protesting segregation. Leading the march are Martin Luther King Jr. and Rabbi Abraham Joshua Heschel. Arm in arm. Flanked by ministers—black and white—and social activists—black and white—and crowds behind them—black and white. They expressed solidarity in their resistance of injustice. What they did, because it turned into photos seen in the world, told the story of the call for racial reconciliation and integration.

I will never forget the day that I opened up the newspaper to see a woman on her knees with her hands stretched out, expressing the deep misery of "Why?" Her name was Mary Ann Vecchio. She was a fourteen-year-old runaway. It was Kent State University, May 4, 1970. I was sixteen. The National Guard fired a shot and killed a young man named Jeffrey Miller. The Vietnam conflict was being protested across the USA (and world). The event told us the Powers had too much power.

In both these events, what the persons *did not do*—use violence—and what they *did do*—march in peaceful protests with a message—told the story.

In Galatians 2, the apostle Paul appeals to events, three of them. The first two are in the passage above and the third one in 2:11–14. **First event:** He takes Titus, "a Greek," to Jerusalem. **Second event:** Paul's message of liberation was affirmed by the most important gospel leaders of his day—Peter (Cephas), James, and John. The two stories, one focusing on *what they did not* do and one on *what they did do*, told the whole story even more than what was written to explain it.

WHAT DID NOT HAPPEN

Fourteen years after Paul's first visit to Jerusalem (see Galatians 1:18–20), Paul returned (2:1). He was sent by the church in Antioch because of a revelation (cf. Acts 11:25–30) with his co-mission workers Barnabas and Titus. Titus was a gentile, a Greek, which means he was uncircumcised. Paul told the leaders there what he was preaching and how they were embodying the message of liberation living in the Christ Era.

The crucial event is this: "Yet not even Titus, who was with me, was compelled to be circumcised, even though he was a Greek" (Gal. 2:3). Circumcision was the sign of covenant membership (Gen. 17). It was, Genesis tells us, "an everlasting covenant" between God and Israel (17:13). Those in the community who choose not to be circumcised break the covenant (17:14). This is in the Bible for Paul's critics in Galatia, and you can bet they were quoting it the way my father quoted the King James Bible. Gentile *converts* to Judaism were circumcised. It was for them what baptism is for Christians. In an Old Testament apocryphal book called Judith, we read of a man named Achior who turned to Israel's God in faith and was circumcised and thus "admitted to the community of Israel" (Judith 14:10). Those who participated in Judaism but didn't undergo circumcision were called **Godfearers**. As Peter preached the gospel to the gentile Cornelius and those who were with him, "the Holy Spirit came on all who heard the message," seen in their speaking in tongues (Acts 10:44–46). They are then baptized (10:47–48), and Peter goes away. I'm guessing you didn't notice something. Paul's critics and some believers in Jerusalem surely noticed that Peter did not require circumcision of this gentile convert!

Not requiring Titus to be circumcised is the event that tells the story that converts to Jesus are free from that ancient practice. A new community was being formed with a new rite of entry: baptism. What *did not happen* tells the story of shifting from the Moses Era into the Christ Era. Paul upends the demand of his critics that gentiles who come into the faith without circumcision are Godfearers and not converts. No, Paul says, all that is needed is faith in Christ formalized in baptism. If circumcision, which embodies full observance of the law of Moses, was not required for Titus, then surely it wasn't a requirement for anyone, and Paul grins, stating implicitly that the Jerusalem leaders were in his corner on this one.

In fact, a discussion occurred about Titus. Paul calls the proponents of the rite for Titus "false believers" or "false siblings" and, to use the term of David deSilva, they weaseled their way into the gathering, their purpose being "to spy on the freedom we have in Christ" (Gal. 2:4). He ramps it up more than one notch when he says they did this "to make us slaves." Which is a way of saying moving from the Christ Era back to the Moses Era! Paul refuses to back down to sustain "the truth of the gospel" (2:5).

Events matter and can tell the story. In this case, what *did not happen* and thus what *was not required* told the story by embodying this shift from the Moses Era to the Christ Era. This was the perfect chance for the leaders in Jerusalem to require the rite. They didn't because they knew it was not required. To make it clear, this is like a Baptist not requiring baptism or a Catholic not requiring mass.

Some churches don't require what other churches do. Some say, You don't have to read this translation. Some say, You don't have to believe in one form of Christian theology or you don't have to belong to that political party or you don't have to be white or you don't have to be of this social class to be in our family. Instead, it is what they *don't do and don't require* that tells the story that "Anyone accepted by Christ is good enough for us." Some churches don't permit women to be elders or deacons or preach or teach. What they *don't do or don't permit* also tells the story.

WHAT DID HAPPEN

I like the next paragraph in this passage for an odd reason. After arguing very hard for his total independence from the Jerusalem authorities in chapter one, Paul shifts. Truth be told, he says with a wink, wink and a nod, nod, "By the way, the major leaders all embraced my liberation message!" He didn't get his message from them, and he didn't need their endorsement, but, now that you bring it up, he tells them, they did validate my message. He appeals to their status: "those who were held in high esteem" (2:6; see also 2:2) and "those esteemed to be pillars" (2:9). He names them, and everyone agrees these are the major players: Peter (Cephas), James, and John. He makes it clear again their status doesn't matter to him because his message is from God (2:6: "whatever they were makes no difference to me"). He states that "they added nothing to his message"—backing up to what they *did not do*. He then states what they *did do*:

1. "they recognized" (2:7),
2. that "God . . . was also at work in me as an apostle to the Gentiles" (2:8),
3. that they "gave me and Barnabas the right hand of fellowship" (2:9) by endorsing the "grace [gift] given to me" (2:9),
4. they "agreed" on equal but separate missions (2:9),
5. and they asked him to find support for the poor in Jerusalem (2:10).

Each of these actions alone embodies official endorsement of the Pauline mission. Again, we keep his mission in mind: preaching the gospel to gentiles, forming churches made up of Judean and gentile believers, and not requiring gentile converts to Jesus to observe the whole law of Moses. The apostles of Jerusalem's church—and this is as close as the church got to the Vatican in the first century—endorsed and embraced the Pauline gospel mission. Paul agreed to what became a life passion, raising funds for the poor of Jerusalem (McKnight), which demonstrated the unity of the church. One can read about this passion in 1 Corinthians 16:1–4; 2 Corinthians 8–9; and Romans 15:25–31.

We experience embodied affirmations of a person as endorsements of their ministry. In the spring of 2021, our local church, Church of the Redeemer, ordained Amanda Holm Rosengren. After she spent a decade leading us in worship, preaching, and pastoring our church, along with our rector Jay Greener, a bishop from Rwanda came to our church, laid hands on her, and publicly endorsed her as a minister of the Word and Sacrament. What he did and what we did—not a few joyous tears appearing—told the story of her calling, her giftedness, and our belief that God calls Jews and gentiles, slave and free, and both women and men into the ministry. What we did mattered.

Events can tell the whole story. The event of not requiring Titus to be circumcised and the event of endorsing Paul's mission tells the story that gentile believers don't have to observe the law of Moses. Therefore, the critics of Paul who are persuading and even coercing (2:3, 14; 6:12) gentile believers to undergo Israel's covenant rite are wrong about the very truth of the gospel!

QUESTIONS FOR REFLECTION AND APPLICATION

1. If events can tell the whole story, what are the important events in this passage that tell the story of what God required of gentile believers?

2. What was the difference between converts to Judaism and Godfearers?

3. Were you surprised by the telling of Cornelius's conversion here? Why or why not? Had you ever considered the importance of what Peter *did not do*? How does this detail impact your view of that narrative?

4. What "events that tell the whole story" stand out in your memory of your own lifetime, such as the examples given in the opening of this chapter?

5. Baptism replaces circumcision as the sign of conversion for Christians. What was your baptism experience like? What did you see, feel, hear, and believe?

FOR FURTHER READING

https://www.kansascity.com/entertainment/arts -culture/article250930469.html

https://www.huffpost.com/entry/martin-luther-king -abraham-heschel_b_8929718

David deSilva, *Galatians*, New International Commentary on the New Testament (Grand Rapids: Wm. B. Eerdmans, 2018).

Scot McKnight, *Pastor Paul* (Grand Rapids: Brazos, 2019), 83–99.

Tom Schreiner, "Circumcision," in *Dictionary of Paul and His Letters*, 2nd ed. (Downers Grove, IL: IVP, 2022).

THE TABLE OF LIBERATION

Galatians 2:11–21

[11] When Cephas came to Antioch, I opposed him to his face, because he stood condemned. [12] For before certain men came from James, he used to eat with the Gentiles. But when they arrived, he began to draw back and separate himself from the Gentiles because he was afraid of those who belonged to the circumcision group. [13] The other Jews joined him in his hypocrisy, so that by their hypocrisy even Barnabas was led astray.[14] When I saw that they were not acting in line with the truth of the gospel, I said to Cephas in front of them all, "You are a Jew, yet you live like a Gentile and not like a Jew. How is it, then, that you force Gentiles to follow Jewish customs?

[15] "We who are Jews by birth and not sinful Gentiles [16] know that a person is not justified by the works of the law, but by faith in Jesus Christ. So we, too, have put our faith in Christ Jesus that we may be justified by faith in Christ and not by the works of the law, because by the works of the law no one will be justified.

[17] But if, in seeking to be justified in Christ, we Jews find

ourselves also among the sinners, doesn't that mean that Christ promotes sin? Absolutely not! [18] If I rebuild what I destroyed, then I really would be a lawbreaker. [19] "For through the law I died to the law so that I might live for God. [20] I have been crucified with Christ and I no longer live, but Christ lives in me. The life I now live in the body, I live by faith in the Son of God, who loved me and gave himself for me. [21] I do not set aside the grace of God, for if righteousness could be gained through the law, Christ died for nothing!"

Some events determine the course of history. Only a handful of events in the mission of the apostles fit the bill of big events, and what happened with Peter and Paul in Antioch (Syria) is one of them. Along with the Council of Jerusalem (Acts 15), Paul confronting Peter over conditions of who eats with whom shaped the church's practice of open table fellowship. Eating in that world embodied equality, so sitting down with another was a public statement that the other person is "in Christ," too.

In 1521, at the Diet of Worms—an assembly in the city of Worms, pronounced "Vōrms"—Martin Luther was challenged to renounce his theological stance that challenged Europe's Catholic establishment. Luther had been declaring the gospel for more than four years, but this was a trial, and he was summoned before the council to deny what he was teaching or else. These are his words:

Unless I am convicted by Scripture and plain reason—I do not accept the authority of popes or councils, for they have contradicted each other—my conscience is captive to the Word of God. I cannot and will not recant anything, for to go against conscience is neither right nor safe. God help me. Amen. [Someone later added "Here I stand, I cannot do otherwise."] (Bainton)

He refused to renounce his teachings, was soon escorted by a band of friends to the Wartburg Castle, and the rest is history. The Lutheran movement exploded throughout Europe and before long was joined by John Calvin's Geneva (Switzerland) Reformation and the more radical reformers, including the Anabaptists under Menno Simons. Protestantism today is what it is because of Luther's momentous event.

Most momentous events are not simply an event. Decisions and actions and responses and oppositions and personalities and politics crystallize into a moment that shakes time and shapes the future. This event with Peter is one such event. Paul had been preaching for as many as two decades; Peter had been doing the same. Paul had more *chutzpah* than Peter, Peter had more politics in his bones—Peter cared more about Jerusalem than did Paul. Paul describes it as a table event (2:11–14) and then Paul explains the gospel of liberation (2:15–21). Paul will get complex in the second part of this passage, and we will not be able to enter into all the discussions. The big picture, however, will come into focus.

THE TABLE EVENT

In Antioch, an early missionary hotspot, Judean and gentile believers are eating with one another. I doubt they were eating pork BBQ, but they were together. Peter joins them at the table—singing and talking and telling stories and eating and enjoying one another. Then "certain men from James" arrive and (Paul says) Peter was scared of the "circumcision group," or put a little less delicately, the guys with blades. If these two groups are the same, we have a contingent arriving that claims to represent the mother church. Whether they claim they are from James or whether they are actually from James is not clear. Remember, James has just endorsed Paul's mission in Galatians 2:1–10. When the guys with blades arrive, Peter has second thoughts about eating in such a mixed fellowship. Paul describes Peter's action as separating himself from the gentiles (2:12). Perhaps when the meal was served, he chose to separate. This is nothing if it is not "separate but equal." The action of an eminent apostle led other Judean believers to join him, and now we have two churches, one for Judean believers and one for gentile believers. We dare not look down on anyone here. There is a chasm between conservative and progressive Christians today, with some thinking the others can't even be Christians! So potent is this separation today that many can't even talk about it in the very church where it needs to be overcome! In our passage so powerful was the contingent's presence that Paul's closest companion (at the time), Barnabas, "was led astray" by this "hypocrisy" (2:14). We are to remember that observance of the law of Moses led many Jews not to eat with gentiles (deSilva, 201–202). Their defense? "Ever read Leviticus?!" (We need, perhaps, also to express some affirmation of Peter for his courage to engage in mixed table fellowship.)

Here's a way of making all this into an image. Plan A in the mission of Paul was a mixed fellowship of Judean (J) and gentile (G) believers, of men (M) and women (W), of slaves (S) and free (Fr) (Gal. 3:28). The contingent from Jerusalem formed into Plan B, where a wall of separation formed into two tables—Judean believers at one table and gentile believers at a second table. Men did not separate themselves from women and the free did not segregate themselves from slaves. But it was Plan B. Plan A was disrupted.

PLAN A

J-M	G-W	J-W	G-M	J-M	G-W	J-W	G-M
G-S	J-Fr	G-Fr	J-S	G-S	J-Fr	G-Fr	J-S

PLAN B

J-S	J-W	J-S	J-Fr	||	G-S	G-Fr	G-S	G-Fr
J-M	J-W	J-Fr	J-S	||	G-W	G-M	G-M	G-W

When Paul hears about Plan B, he explodes with an emotional intensity rarely seen in the New Testament. The pope called Luther a heretic, and Paul gets very close to doing the same when he pins the term "hypocrisy" on Peter and Barnabas. He explains that what they are doing utterly breaks down the gospel and the mission of God in fulfilling the promise to Abraham. As N. T. Wright puts it, "A new day had dawned. Any attempt to draw the lines in the old place, by keeping separate tables for Judean Jesus-followers and gentile Jesus-followers, meant turning back the clock to the 'present evil age' instead of boldly living in 'the age to come,' now inaugurated by Jesus' resurrection and the gift of the Spirit" (*Galatians*, 109).

Perhaps we need to pause for time with Peter. Turn in your Bible to Acts 10, read that whole chapter, and then ask yourself this: How could the man who had such a powerful encounter with God—a magnificent vision—and who preached the gospel to a gentile named Cornelius and who saw the Spirit come down on that group of gentiles and who then just asked them to get baptized . . . how could that man do what he did here in Antioch? Acts 11:1–2, by the way, tells us that when Peter got to Jerusalem, the circumcision group was not happy with him. Acts 11:18 says he silenced that group, and they praised God for gentile conversions—but it apparently didn't stick. Maybe our time with Peter can lead us to ponder how hard it is to maintain a life of liberation. For most of us it takes time.

One of the Bible verses you might just write at the top of the page of this book is Galatians 3:28, and I recommend doing it either in large letters or all upper case. These four lines explain Paul's mission and his motto for each congregation: a fellowship of equals even though it is a fellowship of differents.

> There is neither Jew nor Gentile,
>> neither slave nor free,
>> nor is there male and female,
>> for you are all one in Christ Jesus.

Paul got in Peter's face. (I paraphrase, but the tone gets it right.) Because Peter created a church division, Paul opposes Peter "in front of them all." Paul in good rhetorical fashion asks a question that pins the gospel to the wall for all, and I paraphrase again: "If you, Peter, have been acting like a gentile in mixing with gentiles at the table, how can you now coerce"—he uses a very strong term—"The gentiles to judaize?" That is, Peter was in the Christ Era when eating with everyone, but now he's making people back up to the Moses Era! (As for that very strong term, there were times when Jews physically forced gentiles in their country to get circumcised if they wanted to live in their midst. This sounds like that.)

A long time ago we—the church—began living in Plan B. A long time ago we (white) Christians segregated ourselves from "Brown" Christians, as Robert Chao Romero describes it. A long time ago, we stole their land and avoided their holistic gospel and broke off the opportunity for the gospel of liberation. We did this a long time ago, and every Sunday when we gather without our Brown brothers and sisters in our midst, or we in their midst, we deny Paul's gospel by living in Plan B. In Plan B, we live into a theology that does not rescue us from our divisions, however they are based. As Romero puts it in his brilliant book *Brown Church*,

> Brown Theologians throughout the centuries . . . challenged this narrow and unbiblical view of the gospel and have proclaimed that Jesus came to save, redeem, and transform every aspect of our lives and the world. His salvation extends over all of God's good creation, which has become twisted and corrupted as a consequence of sin. This includes everything distorted and broken in

147

our world—whether personal, familial, social, or global. Nothing is left out.

So, let's confess our Plan B life. Let's lament our Plan B system. Let's invite Brown brothers and sisters, and let's listen to their invitations to us. Plan A, the Plan of God for the Christ Era, knows no other way.

The Explanation

Paul now steps back, writing at some remove from that event, and explains his eruption. He speaks now to Peter and the Judean experience of conversion from the Moses Era to the Christ Era. The shift occurred for both Peter and Paul when they trusted Jesus as Messiah. That act of faith was one in which they said the Moses Era was now fulfilled in the Christ Era, and that meant for them that the law of Moses had served its purpose for them.

When Paul uses "works of the law," we need to hear this term along the line of the Promise Era to the Moses Era to the Christ Era. Those "works" are how one was to live in the Moses Era, but in the Christ Era "works of the law" become obsolete. Many have read "works of the law" as humans attempting to earn favor with God on the basis of works. That is, many have read it as "works righteousness" or "meritorious righteousness." Scholars in the last fifty years have put that understanding to bed. Jews did not think they had to earn their way with God; they were the elect of God on the basis of God's prior grace in forming a covenant with them. They didn't go to bed wondering if they were going to be saved if they died during the night any more than you wonder if you will wake up in the morning a member of a different nationality or ethnicity. Instead, when Paul uses "works of the law," he is pointing to these acts that distinguished Jews from gentiles: circumcision, food laws (read through Leviticus 11), and Sabbath (Dunn, Thomas). The singular event of Peter withdrawing from gentiles at table is the very thing Paul means by "works of the law." Since the gentile believers did not follow Judean food laws and were not circumcised, the contingent put pressure on Peter and Barnabas, and they caved.

Let's not pat ourselves on the back too soon. Any number of acts—from what we eat to what we wear to what translation we read to which pastor we cherish the most to which denomination or church we belong to—any of these may not be moving into the Moses Era but they function in our fellowship as the "works of the law" functioned in Antioch. They can be used to mark people as accepted or not accepted (to us).

This passage's complications now arise. Paul says that he and Peter learned that being right with God—"justified" (2:16, 17)—was because of *faith*, not "works of the law." The Christ Era in Paul's timeline is when the Christ-kind-of-faith came (3:23). Being among "sinners," that is, gentiles (2:17; see 2:15), does not make Christ an agent of sin. One of my favorite complications in this passage is this. In 2:18, Paul speaks to Peter in terms of the first person: "If I [Paul and Peter] rebuild what I destroyed" means Peter backing up to the Moses Era as a requirement for gentile believers. It means rebuilding that wall that had been knocked down at the cross and resurrection. It means the wall embodied in Plan B above. In fact, Paul says "I" have died to the Era of Moses when "I" was "crucified with Christ" in the Christ Era. That "I" of the Judean sole election privilege is now over, and Christ is now living in this "I." The whole life is now lived by faith in Jesus, who came to rescue this "I" (2:20). He now responds to what must have been a routine criticism of Paul. In moving from the Era of Moses to the Era of Christ, Paul is not abandoning the grace of God at work in the previous eras. No, the works of the law in the Moses Era never brought the grace now known in Christ.

This event in Antioch changed history for the early church. While the struggle continued no doubt from community to community and from house church to house church, the pattern was set. Gospel life in the Christ Era means mixed table fellowship.

Separation at the table denies the gospel.

QUESTIONS FOR REFLECTION AND APPLICATION

1. Explain the Christian ideal of open table fellowship.

THE TABLE OF LIBERATION

2. After Peter's boldness in standing up for gentile believers like Cornelius, and his apparent practice of table fellowship with gentiles, what caused him to change his mind and step into hypocrisy? What do you imagine were the pressures on Peter?

3. What are the works of the law, and how did they function in the Moses Era and then in the Christ Era?

4. Why do you think Paul used such strong language and intense rhetoric in opposing Peter? Have you ever challenged a fellow believer in a similar way? What led to your decision to do so?

5. Do you experience a Plan B table seating arrangement in your church or community? What are the dividing lines? Which groups or types of people would you not want to eat with?

FOR FURTHER READING

Roland Bainton, *Here I Stand: A Life of Martin Luther* (Nashville: Abingdon, 2013), 192.

Daniel DeSilva, *Galatians*, New International Commentary on the New Testament (Grand Rapids: Wm. B. Eerdmans, 2018), 198–203 for a good discussion of the mealtime challenge.

James D. G. Dunn, *The Theology of Paul the Apostle* (Grand Rapids: Wm. B. Eerdmans, 1998), 354–366.

Scot McKnight, *A Fellowship of Differents* (Grand Rapids: Zondervan, 2016).

Robert Chao Romero, *Brown Church* (Downers Grove, IL: IVP, 2020), 12.

Matthew Thomas, *Paul's "Works of the Law" in the Perspective of Second-Century Reception* (Downers Grove: IVP, 2020).

EXPERIENCES OF
LIBERATION

Galatians 3:1–5

¹ You foolish Galatians! Who has bewitched you? Before your very eyes Jesus Christ was clearly portrayed as crucified. ² I would like to learn just one thing from you: Did you receive the Spirit by the works of the law, or by believing what you heard? ³ Are you so foolish? After beginning by means of the Spirit, are you now trying to finish by means of the flesh? ⁴ Have you experienced so much in vain—if it really was in vain? ⁵ So again I ask, does God give you his Spirit and work miracles among you by the works of the law, or by your believing what you heard?

Those three events, one with Titus, one where Paul is endorsed by church leaders, and one with Peter in Antioch, matter because they embody the gospel Paul is preaching. Experiences matter, too.

Paul reported his own experience on the Damascus Road in chapter one, describing it as an experience in which God revealed the Son of God to him. This experience is told three different times in Acts, no doubt indicating how often Paul himself told his story (9:1–19; 22:3–16; 26:9–18). Some propose that much of Paul's theology derives from that eye-twittering conversion experience. The apostle Peter writes about being an eyewitness of the majesty of Jesus when he saw Jesus transfigured, and he finishes with "we were with him on the sacred mountain" (2 Peter 1:16–18). An unforgettable experience. And here's how John summarizes his experiences with Jesus:

> We announce to you what existed from the beginning, what we have heard, what we have seen with our eyes, what we have seen and our hands handled, about the word of life. The life was revealed, and we have seen, and we testify and announce to you the eternal life that was with the Father and was revealed to us. What we have seen and heard, we also announce it to you so that you can have fellowship with us (1 John 1:1–3 CEB).

Some believe we should avoid talking of our experiences and focus on the rational, which is a way of saying (far too often) that experiences and emotions don't matter. A Christian faith shorn of the depth of human experience, which can't be reduced to the rational, contradicts the Bible. From Adam and Eve to John's Revelation, the Bible tells of experience after experience. Because experiences matter.

Experiences embody the faith we confess. No one could ever accuse Paul of avoiding the rational—ever read Romans 7 or Romans 9–11? Or Galatians? But the rational and experiences combine to form us into fully functioning humans. In this passage that opens Galatians 3, Paul appeals to the conversion experiences of the Galatians and asks them, as it were, to look inside and answer his questions *from their experience of God*. His simple question is, "How did it happen?" He only gives them two options: on the basis of observing the law, that is, "works of the law," or on the basis of their trusting Christ? He opens with a double accusation.

Double Accusation

First accusation: they are "foolish" or, uninformed or unthinking or irrational or even ignorant. Second accusation, a question: "Are you *bewitched*?" The Common English Bible translates it, "Who put a spell on you?" The assumptions and practice of putting the evil eye on someone were common in the ancient world. (My grandmother called it "giving someone the daggers," as in, "I sure gave her the daggers!") Paul here describes the deviant teachings of his critics in Galatia. They are using their spells to entrance and deceive.

Four Experiences

The stakes are high, and to counter the spells of the critics, Paul appeals both to events and to four experiences. They were converted to Jesus in dramatic fashion, for Paul speaks of some kind of display when he says they are ones before whose eyes "Jesus Christ was clearly portrayed as crucified" (3:1). This language emerges from the power of rhetorical persuasion. Somehow that early gospel preaching created vivid images in the experiences of the Galatians. It is not hard to imagine that Paul had mastered descriptions of the suffering of Jesus as a victim of brutality.

Let's not lose where we are with Paul. His intent is clear. He wants the Galatians to embrace the gospel of liberation from the law because of the arrival in God's plan of the Christ Era. Therefore, redemption and standing in the people of God cannot be based on the "works of the law" because those are habits of the Moses Era.

Paul asks the question "How did it happen?" by asking about four of their experiences. If they answer as Paul wants, it'll be game, set, match.

Experience #1: Reception. The experience Paul points to is reception of the Spirit (Gal. 3:2). How did they get the Spirit? On the basis of the works of the law (no) or on the basis of the experience of trusting Christ (yes)? Their Spirit-reception experience was most probably like those in Acts, which were sometimes accompanied by laying on of hands (Acts 8:14–20; 9:17; 19:6) and speaking in tongues (2:1–4; 19:6) or a thunderous shaking (4:31) or increased boldness or prophesying (4:31; 19:6) or some falling down because of the Spirit upon them (10:44–48).

Experience #2: Growth. He moves on in their faith journey to growth. Having begun in the Spirit (3:2), he asks if they are progressing and reaching maturity in the Christian life "by means of the flesh (3:3)," another term Paul connects to the Moses Era. The answer is no; it's all in the Spirit.

Experience #3: Suffering. This question requires an understanding of the term behind the NIV's "experienced"

(3:4). The Greek term is *paschō* and refers to suffering in every other occurrence in Paul's letters (1 Cor. 12:26; 2 Cor. 1:6; Phil. 1:29; 1 Thess. 2:14; 2 Thess. 1:5; 2 Tim. 1:12). One finds evidence of persecution in Galatians 4:29 as well. He asks them—even if it refers only to the general experiences of 3:1–3—has been in vain? If they step back into the Moses Era, they experienced all this or they suffered all this in vain. If they stay in the Christ Era, the suffering will prove to be of value. Again, he's basing his argument on their experiences, most likely suffering for Christ.

Experience #4: Miracles. His fourth question about experience concerns the presence of miracles. Miracles were (and sometimes still are) a common experience of Christians (Twelftree).

Again, it's about the power of the Spirit present in their experiences in which they see miracles occurring (3:5). Did they experience these on the basis of a Moses Era response ("works of the law") or a Christ Era response ("faith")? Everyone now say, "faith."

One time I read through Acts carefully and highlighted in yellow every time the Spirit was mentioned, and if it was an experience of the Spirit, I highlighted the entire passage. I was surprised, and not a little happy about it, to see how Spirit-drenched Acts is. I also drew red lines around every passage about persecution, which was another solid list of passages. Putting my markers down, I realize again how experiential the Christian faith was and remains.

The Galatians' experiences of the supernatural, when analyzed rationally, demonstrate that God's redemptive liberation comes by faith, not by the works of the law. Experiences mattered to Paul, so much so that he could appeal to them in the very heart of this rationally drenched letter.

QUESTIONS FOR REFLECTION AND APPLICATION

1. Why do experiences matter in the Christian life? How do experiences embody faith?

2. How do Paul, Peter, and John talk about their experiences with Jesus?

3. What are Paul's two accusations against the Galatians, and what do they mean?

4. How do you think Paul's critics or those who sided with his critics responded to Paul's questions?

5. Consider the four experiences of the Galatians that Paul brings up to them: reception of the Spirit, growth by the Spirit, suffering, and miracles. Which of your own experiences with God do these categories remind you of? Tell about an experience that embodies your faith.

FOR FURTHER READING

Graham Twelftree, *Paul and the Miraculous* (Grand Rapids: Baker Academic, 2013), 187–191.

SIX SCRIPTURES
OF LIBERATION

Galatians 3:6–14

⁶ [1] So also Abraham "believed God, and it was credited to him as righteousness." *⁷ Understand, then, that those who have faith are children of Abraham.*

⁸ [2] Scripture foresaw that God would justify the Gentiles by faith, and announced the gospel in advance to Abraham: "All nations will be blessed through you." *⁹ So those who rely on faith are blessed along with Abraham, the man of faith.*

¹⁰ [3] For all who rely on the works of the law are under a curse, as it is written: "Cursed is everyone who does not continue to do everything written in the Book of the Law."

¹¹ [4] Clearly no one who relies on the law is justified before God, because "the righteous will live by faith."

¹² [5] The law is not based on faith; on the contrary, it says, "The person who does these things will live by them."

¹³ [6] Christ redeemed us from the curse of the law by becoming a curse for us, for it is written: "Cursed is everyone who is hung on a pole." *¹⁴ He redeemed us in order that the blessing given to Abraham might come to the Gentiles through Christ Jesus, so that by faith we might receive the promise of the Spirit.*

E vents matter. Experiences matter. Scriptures matter. We are all tempted to quote a Bible verse and think we are done with it. One of pastor-author Dan Kimball's rules for Bible reading is, "Never read a Bible verse." What he means is never read one verse in isolation from its paragraph, chapter, book, and the context of the storyline of the Bible. One can say this just as quickly about topics. You can pinch between two fingers some line about wealth for obedience from Deuteronomy 28 and run roughshod over Job and Jesus and James because they offer nuance upon nuance about poverty for the one who follows hard after God. Paul knows how to read a Bible verse in the storyline, and he also knows how to work a topic in the whole of the Bible. He does it here and teaches us how to read the Bible well.

Here's our problem. Even when someone knows the Bible well and can amass a collection of ideas and verses on a theme, we may simply not want to listen. We are all comfortable in our ways. Change is hard. Big changes are even harder. They cause learning anxiety because we recognize the changes that may occur. Paul is asking for the biggest change of all: to get people to read the Bible, not through the law of Moses but through the promise given to Abraham. It's the same Bible with a massively different approach. I've watched this play out in my lifetime. I saw people shift their view about the rapture and tribulation, about the King James Bible when the NIV came along, about the light shed on the Bible when the Dead Sea Scrolls were discovered, about changing perspectives on Paul, about women preaching and teaching and pastoring in the church, about how to sing and worship in churches, about what pastors are to wear, and during COVID-19 about online eucharist . . . and every one of these shifts, and plenty more, were resisted by the old guard and not always for good reasons.

That's Paul's very situation, and so he turns his argu ments about events and experiences to the Bible itself. In Galatians 3:6–14, he quotes Genesis 15:6, then Genesis 12:3, then Deuteronomy 27:26, then Habakkuk 2:4, then Leviticus 18:5, and then lastly he returns to Deuteronomy, this time to 21:23. You and I can use online Bible searches or pick up our Bible programs—I use Accordance—and type in a word or two (say "righteousness" or "faith" or "gentiles" or "blessing"), and our programs will pop up the Bible references on a screen. Not so with Paul. He had his Bible in his memory.

You might ask, why did Paul turn to Abraham? Probably because the critics anchored their defense in Abraham—the one who believed and who was circumcised. Right there in Genesis 12, 15, and 17. Paul turned to Abraham because Abraham (1) was *justified*, a central idea for Paul, (2) because Abraham's approval by God was based on *faith*, and (3) because Abraham's justification occurs *not on the basis of works, that is, his circumcision.* Paul grabs the very example his opponents used and beats them at their own game: using the Bible!

CONTEXT ONE
MORE TIME

Context matters all the time. In Galatia some gentile believers are convinced, or have been convinced by Judean believers, that to be fully devoted followers of Jesus they must embrace the law of Moses. For Paul this means moving back in time from the Christ Era to the Moses Era. They are not appealing to preferences, the way you or I may appeal to Reformed or Lutheran or Anglican theology, no matter how important such may be to us. For them, this shift to the Moses Era expresses *what God wants for every human*. They have ramped this up. It's what God *requires for redemption*.

Remember this: what we value supremely, we talk about and emphasize and urge others to embrace. When we value something that is religious, we bring God into what we value. So much so that people believe what we value is what God values. This is especially the case with those who teach and preach the Bible, and also for moms and dads. If we value "works of the law" or "liberation from the law," we are announcing what God wants. If we think it is practicing miracles or speaking in tongues or studying the Bible every day or going on prayer retreats or attending every Sunday service (not Saturday night's service) or being baptized by immersion or adhering to the teachings of some particular preacher or author or theologian . . . we are embodying what we think God approves most. Actions matter.

Four Words

Some words matter more than other words. Paul uses four of his favorites in this passage. The most important word is **righteousness**. This term translates the Greek term *dikaios* and comes from the Hebrew term *tsedeq*, the words being major moral categories in the Bible. To be righteous is to be acceptable to God. A twist happens in English that we need to untwist: the noun *dikaios* becomes a verb as *dikaioō*, and that word is translated "justify." So, justify is to be "righted" or "made righteous" or "declared in the right" by an act of God. If you look at our chart on page 105, you will see that justification and righteousness are not found in the Moses Era. That, my friends, is Paul's biggest point in this letter.

1. The second word Paul latches onto is **faith**. Another twist occurs that needs untwisting: *faith* translates *pistis* and the verbal form is *pisteuō*, but it gets translated "to believe," and that means "believe" and "faith" are identical. In the Bible, faith means the act of trusting Christ (faith)
2. the ongoing acts of trusting (faithfulness), and
3. the content of what we believe as Christians (the faith).

When Lauren Daigle sings her beautiful song "You Say,"[1] in which she resists the many false voices and lies of

---

1. Lauren Daigle, "You Say," Copyright © 2018 CentricSongs (SESAC) See You at the Pub (SESAC) (adm. at CapitolCMGPublishing.com) / Flychild

comparison that she hears, she sings out, "I believe" you, God, in who "you say" I am. How is she using the term "believe" here?

The third word is **nations** (or gentiles). One of the promises God gave to Abraham was "and all the peoples on earth will be blessed through you" (Genesis 12:3). Israel's vocation was to spread knowledge of their covenant God to the whole world, something they didn't do. Their only true missionary, Jonah, was a grump. Through the Spirit, God called Paul to a mission to the nations—to Romans and Greeks and barbarians and Scythians and even Green Bay Packers and New York Yankees fans! Sorry for that, let's move on.

A fourth word, the **promise-blessing**, returns to the promise to Abraham. Gentiles would inherit that world-encompassing blessing (Genesis 12). This word is a picnic basket of goodies. Inside it one finds justification and reconciliation and redemption and liberation and church and Spirit and all sorts of condiments, too!

Get these four words right, and you've got Paul in your grip, and Paul was teaching the Galatians how to read the Bible through God's promise to Abraham.

SIX SCRIPTURES

To launch his Scripture argument, which continues all the way through the end of chapter four, Paul collects six

Publishing (SESAC) / So Essential Tunes (SESAC) / Fellow Ships Music (SESAC) (admin at EssentialMusicPublishing.com).

Scriptures to bolster his four words, which I keep in bold for illustration. If you keep our timeline from Promise to Law to Christ handy, everything in this passage falls in place like a mama robin plopping into her nest.

First, in 3:6 he cites Genesis 15:6 and so reminds the Galatians that the granddaddy of them all, Abraham, was made right with God by **faith**. God **promised** him nothing less than the **gentile** world in Genesis 12:1–3, but he remained childless, and he speaks with God with nothing less than the obvious question: "Where's the baby?" God shows him the stars and **promises** his heirs will be that numerous. "Abram **believed** the LORD," that is, trusted God, and God "credited it to him as **righteousness**" (15:6). If we are all children of Abraham (Gal. 3:7), it is because we **trust** in God as did Abraham. If Abraham was **made right** by **faith**, then **gentiles** are. Paul will develop this even more in Romans 4.

Second, at Galatians 3:8, Paul backs up to Genesis 12. God's **promise** from the very beginning included Israel going to the **gentiles**, to the nations. But notice the subtle shift Paul makes in 3:9 above. If it was to Abraham that the **gentile promise** was made, and Abraham was **made right by faith**, the **gentiles** will gain this **blessing** the same way: by **faith**. Again, not by works of the law but by **trusting** Christ as God's agent of redemption.

Third, Paul turns "works of the law" against the pro-circumcision party by showing what happens to those who rely on the law (3:10). Again, our chart shows the Moses Era brings not **righteousness**, not **justification**, and not the **blessing** but a curse. Paul turns to the Bible's major commitment service in Deuteronomy 27. Moses tells Israel to cross the River Jordan and there write the words of the covenant law on plastered stones. Then they are to divide the tribes into two groups, one group announcing **blessings** for obedience and the other curses for disobedience. The curses are for idolatries and disrespect of parents and stealing property lines and deception of the blind when walking and injustice for "the foreigner, the fatherless or the widow," and also for sexual immoralities and perversions and murders and then the final one sums it all up: "Cursed is anyone who does not uphold the words of this law by carrying them out" (27:26). Commitment to the law leads backward and not forward. In the Christ Era, there is the empowerment of the Holy Spirit, blessings, life, and righteousness.

Fourth, fifth, and sixth tie the threads of the first three into a knot (Gal. 3:11–14). The law cannot make a person **righteous** because the prophet said, "the righteous will live by faith," and the law is not based on **faith** but on *doing the works of the law.* And the law has the power to curse those living under it. But there is good news. The cursed— which means those in the Moses Era and those who want to return to it—have been liberated by Christ. He became that very curse when he was crucified (3:13). Paul cites Deuteronomy 21:23's statement that anyone who is hung on a pole, one of the forms of crucifixion, is cursed by God. Jesus absorbed the power of the law to curse.

The great, great, great news of this string of quotations from the Old Testament? Now the **blessings**, the other half of the tribes of Israel in Deuteronomy 28, can come to **gentiles** because the lid on the covenant is lifted from those who do "works of the law" to those who exercise **faith**.

It is all in those three, yea four, words: **righteousness** comes by **faith** with the **blessing** given to Abraham and **gentiles**. Four words, six texts.

Paul knows the Scriptures about liberation from the law in the Christ Era.

QUESTIONS FOR REFLECTION AND APPLICATION

1. What example does Paul set for us of how to read the Scriptures well?

2. How does Paul use his memorized knowledge of Scripture to change the lens of reading from the Moses lens to the Abrahamic promise lens?

3. What are Paul's four major words in this section of Galatians, and how does he use them to weave together and explain his six Scripture references?

4. What major changes have you witnessed in church culture, belief, or mindset over your lifetime?

5. Can you think of anything you value that you have attributed to God valuing, and passed it on to others as a requirement for faith? What map does this chapter give you for addressing that in yourself?

FOR FURTHER READING

Dan Kimball, *How (Not) to Read the Bible* (Grand Rapids: Zondervan, 2021), 39–57.

THREE QUESTIONS ABOUT LIBERATION

Galatians 3:26–29

²⁶ So in Christ Jesus you are all children of God through faith, ²⁷ for all of you who were baptized into Christ have clothed yourselves with Christ. ²⁸ There is neither Jew nor Gentile, neither slave nor free [liberated], nor is there male and female, for you are all one in Christ Jesus. ²⁹ If you belong to Christ, then you are Abraham's seed, and heirs according to the promise. [Note: I have chosen to add "liberated" in brackets in 3:28.]

Special Note to the Reader: For the reflection on Galatians 3:15–25, see pp. 100–112.

Events, experiences, Scriptures—each matters. Theological foundations matter, too, and in this passage, Paul explores the powerful impact of "in Christ" to sort out the problem at Galatia. Paul's critics must have claimed that gentiles who did not go all the way in their faith to embrace the law of Moses were not fully committed

Christians. Maybe even that the gentiles weren't even in Christ yet. Probably that they were half-converts.

Have you ever experienced someone suggesting that your faith was incomplete because you had not yet spoken in tongues or had not embraced some form of Christian theology or had not joined the right church? I have. It was bewildering. We could call it "theological gaslighting."

Notice how often Paul asserts *who* is acceptable to God. Read these verses from chapters three and four, and I italicize the words that state who are the people of God (see deSilva, 279):

Understand, then, that *those who have faith* are children of Abraham (3:7).

So *those who rely on faith* are blessed along with Abraham, the man of faith (3:9).

For all of you who were baptized into Christ have clothed yourselves with Christ (3:27).

If you belong to Christ, then you are Abraham's seed, and heirs according to the promise (3:29).

Because you are his sons, *God sent the Spirit of his Son into our hearts*, the Spirit who calls out, *"Abba, Father."* So you are no longer a slave, *but God's child*; and since you are his child, God has made *you also an heir* (4:6–7).

For it is written that Abraham had two sons, one by the slave woman and *the other by the free woman* (4:22).

Now you, brothers and sisters, like Isaac, are children of promise (4:28).

Therefore, brothers and sisters, we are not children of the slave woman, *but of the free woman* (4:31).

Paul's critics' claim is that one must do the "works of the law," those stipulations in the law of Moses that most visibly demonstrate a heartfelt embrace of the law, if they want to go hard after God. Their support, of course, is the Bible. Their question can be summed up in these words: "Do you, Paul, think we are to follow the law of Moses or not?"

Paul's questions topple the tables: "Do they believe in Jesus?" and "Are they baptized?" and "Do you embrace all who are in Christ?"

Before we turn to Paul's questions, we need to pause to consider what we are adding to Christ to judge who is fully acceptable and fully devoted. What questions are we asking of others? What translation do you use? Who is your favorite pastor? Which is your political party? Where do you live? What do you think of Critical Race Theory? I'll go full liberation here and say that if any of these questions point to an answer that leads you to exclude someone from being fully devoted, well then, you need to answer Paul's questions yourself. Now's your chance.

Do They Believe in Jesus?

Paul's response, as we sketched in 3:15–25, is the Moses Era has done its job, and we now live in the Christ Era. His claim then is simple and profound. *Everyone in Christ is in.* And how does one get in? Paul sees two dimensions, the first being dominant: by faith. Notice how Paul opens with a fourfold claim that is so quick we may miss how important it is. "So [1] in Christ Jesus [2] you are all [3] children of God [4] through faith" (3:26). We draw attention here only to what has already been discussed. We are saved *by faith*. Not by returning to the Moses Era to do the "works of the law" but by remaining in the Christ Era by trusting.

Who's in the people of God, then? Anyone who believes in Jesus.

ARE THEY BAPTIZED?

Our passage continues with the paradigmatic embodiment of faith, the second dimension of how one enters the people of God, when it says, "For all of you who were *baptized* into Christ" (3:27). There is a tendency for some today to think of baptism here as spiritual baptism, and one can sympathize with a fear that if we're not careful, we'll have a baptism-itself-saves theology. But that's not right either. The faith commitment of the earliest Christians was embodied by baptism in water. There was no such thing as an unbaptized believer, and those who refused baptism did not yet have sufficient faith. Baptism needs to be seen for what it is in the New Testament. The New Testament connects our baptism in water to union with Christ (Rom. 6:1–14; Col. 2:11–12), to the reception of the Spirit (Acts 2:38; 1 Cor. 12:13) and, yes, to forgiveness and redemption (McKnight, *It Takes a Church to*

Baptize). This third point provokes anxiety, so read these verses for yourself:

> Peter replied, "Repent and be baptized, every one of you, in the name of Jesus Christ for the forgiveness of your sins. And you will receive the gift of the Holy Spirit (Acts 2:38).

> And now what are you waiting for? Get up, be baptized and wash your sins away, calling on his name (22:16).

> And that is what some of you were. But you were washed, you were sanctified, you were justified in the name of the Lord Jesus Christ and by the Spirit of our God (1 Cor. 6:11).

Because faith was embodied for all of them in water baptism, they saw their baptism as their moment of redemption. But this is why Paul begins the passage we are discussing with these words: "for all of you who were baptized into Christ have clothed yourselves with Christ" (Gal. 3:27). If you were to ask a first-century Christian, "When were you saved?" the person would most likely say, "I was baptized two years ago." That's how tight baptism and redemption were (and are). Our disconnection fails the test of what the Bible says.

If you are baptized in the baptism that unites with Christ, that prompts the reception of the Spirit, and that leads to redemption, then you are "in Christ," and if you are "in Christ," then you are in the people of God. Bingo! This relationship with Christ is what matters and not works of the law.

Who's in the people of God, then? The ones who are baptized.

Do You Embrace All in Christ?

Galatians 3:28, one of the most quoted lines of the apostle Paul's, deserves being memorized and quoted over and over. There is an edge to Paul's words here. He's pushing back against his critics who think the elective privilege of Israel remains in the Christ Era. Their privilege is put aside for it is eternal (Rom. 11:28–29). The change is that *all in Christ are raised into that elective privilege.* In Christ, Jews are not demoted; gentiles are promoted.

Those who believe, those who are baptized, are "all one in Christ Jesus" (Gal. 3:28). The word "one" is important. There is one God, one Lord (Jesus Christ), one Spirit, one body, one hope, one faith, and one baptism (1 Cor. 8:4–6; Eph. 4:5–6)—and through that one Spirit each one is given a gift for the one body! Paul's claim cuts against how we operate in the church today. If you embrace Christ, you embrace his body, and that means you embrace the whole body because the body is one. We are one. We violate our one God and one Lord and one Spirit—all the ones—when we cut up the body into Baptists, Anglicans, Presbyterians, Methodists, liberals, conservatives, progressives, white, black, brown, wealthy, poor, college-d, and uncollege-d.

That's what was happening in Galatia. One group separated from another when it came to the table based on whether or not the person observed the law of Moses. It went both ways. Gentile believers at times looked down on Judean believers and the reverse (read Rom. 14:1–15:13).

Paul's manifesto points a centuries-long finger at anyone who cuts up the body of Christ. Paul points to three transcendent points of unity in Christ. He begins with *ethnicity*, and he is speaking here of race, ethnicity, social status, and power. He demolishes power structures. In Christ there is no longer "Jew nor Gentile." This does not mean Jews are no longer Jews and gentiles are no longer gentiles and that they become a kind of third race. No, distinctions remain, and those distinctions should be celebrated, but they are transcended in the one body. He demolishes here any claim to superiority, and such claims depend on social location. In Rome, gentiles had more power. In Jerusalem, Jews had more power. No longer was that power to be exercised in Christ.

Second, he turns to another power structure: the freeperson who gained freedom from slavery and the slave who remained powerless in slavery. No longer does this power structure obtain in the church. When Paul sent the slave Onesimus back to his owner, Philemon, he told the owner that Onesimus was to be received "no longer as a slave, but better than a slave, as a dear brother" (Philemon 16). At the same time, he told the slave owners in Colosse to treat their slaves with justice and equality (NIV has "right and fair" at 4:1). The demolition of this power structure demonstrates the radical edge of the first-century churches.

Before moving to the third pair in these power structures, I want to make one short observation: the segregation by Christians on the basis of race or ethnicity rebuilds the very walls Paul has demolished in the first two power structures. If there is neither Jew nor gentile and neither slave nor free, there is to be no power structures built on being white, African American, Asian American, or Latin American (McCaulley, Kim, Romero).

Third, Paul undoes Genesis 1:27, which says, "male and female he created them." In Christ they too are one. Men remain men, women remain women, but that relationship is not equal as the power has been surrendered to Christ. We Christians indwell a hierarchical world shaped by patriarchal ideologies in which women are silenced, suppressed, oppressed, abused, and violated. The development of masculinist ideologies among many Christian conservatives and the justification of it on the basis of a so-called "manhood and womanhood" have recently been exposed as deficient understandings of the Bible and damage-causing social systems (Barr, Byrd, DuMez). These, too, rebuild the walls Paul demolishes in Galatians 3:28.

Paul's question for the Galatians finds its gravity in Galatians 3:28:

- Do you embrace all who are in Christ, who have faith in Christ, who are baptized, on the basis of their relation to Christ?

  or
- Do you embrace only those on your side of the power structures? Or do you embrace them only if they follow your set of convictions?

Who is in the people of God, then? *All* who believe, who are baptized, no matter where they are on the scales of power. Especially those who have been rendered powerless by ethnic privilege, status privilege, and gender privilege.

That's liberation "in Christ."

QUESTIONS FOR REFLECTION AND APPLICATION

1. Who are the people of God according to Paul?

2. What are the two questions Paul uses to determine who is in Christ?

3. What questions are you asking of others that might lead you to exclude someone from being, in your estimation, fully devoted to Christ?

4. Are any of these power differentials or areas of privilege hard for you to overcome?

5. Have you ever experienced someone suggesting that your faith was incomplete? What criteria did they use? How did it make you feel?

FOR FURTHER READING

Beth Allison Barr, *The Making of Biblical Womanhood* (Grand Rapids: Brazos, 2021).

Aimee Byrd, *Recovering from Biblical Manhood and Womanhood* (Grand Rapids: Zonderan, 2020).

Daniel DeSilva, *Galatians*, New International Commentary on the New Testament (Grand Rapids: Wm. B. Eerdmans, 2018).

Kristin Kobes Du Mez, *Jesus and John Wayne* (New York: Norton/Liveright, 2020).

Grace Ji-Sun Kim, *Invisible: Theology and the Experience of Asian American Women* (Minneapolis: Fortress, 2021).

Esau McCaulley, *Reading While Black* (Downers Grove, IL: IVP, 2020).

Scot McKnight, *It Takes a Church to Baptize* (Grand Rapids: Brazos, 2018), 47–62.

Robert Chao Romero, *Brown Church* (Downers Grove, IL: IVP, 2020).

ADOPTION INTO LIBERATION

Galatians 4:1–11

¹ What I am saying is that as long as an heir is underage, he is no different from a slave, although he owns the whole estate. ² The heir is subject to guardians and trustees until the time set by his father. ³ So also, when we were underage, we were in slavery under the elemental spiritual forces of the world. ⁴ But when the set time had fully come, God sent his Son, born of a woman, born under the law, ⁵ to redeem those under the law, that we might receive adoption [into the family]. ⁶ Because you are his sons [and daughters], God sent the Spirit of his Son into our hearts, the Spirit who calls out, "Abba, Father." ⁷ So you are no longer a slave, but God's child; and since you are his child, God has made you also an heir.

⁸ Formerly, when you did not know God, you were slaves to those who by nature are not gods. ⁹ But now that you know God—or rather are known by God—how is it that you are turning back to those weak and miserable forces? Do you wish to be enslaved by them all over again? ¹⁰ You are observing special days and months and seasons and years! [11] *I fear for you, that somehow I have wasted my efforts on you. [***Note:*** I have edited the NIV from "adoption into sonship" in 4:5 into "adoption into the family" and have added "and daughters" to "sons" in 4:6.]*

At one time I drove a small SUV, a Subaru Forester. I enjoyed being a bit higher on the road in my commute. At the same time, Kris commuted in her Toyota Camry to her office. My Subaru was beginning to wear down, so we decided to sell it and purchase another Toyota Camry, one my son was selling. When I began to commute in the "new" Camry, I experienced something I had never noticed. The Camry was so quiet that I realized my Subaru was very noisy. I did not know the buzzzzzzz the car was making until I drove the quieter car. Being who I am, I Googled about it and learned that my previous car was in fact known as noisy.

The language the apostle Paul uses in this passage—slavery, "elemental spiritual forces of the world," and "weak and miserable forces"—was the buzz, but those words were not the language he would have ever used before God invaded his life and shattered his previous way of life. In fact, he was convinced of his own obedience and the law's goodness (cf. Phil. 3:5–6; Stendahl). But his life was flipped inside out on the Road to Damascus, and his theology flipped with it. When Paul discovered the liberating power of the Spirit, a liberation from the Moses Era, he started to describe his past in new terms: it was slavery. The quiet liberation in Christ made him aware of the buzz of the Moses Era. To depict the Moses Era as slavery is powerful language, and powerful language needs to be understood well, or we end up in a swamp of misreadings. Paul is not saying the law was and is in itself enslaving so much as he is saying that life in Christ is so much better and so liberating that his former life is comparable to slavery. The quiet of Christ made him aware of the buzz under the law.

That quiet life of liberation in Christ has at least five dimensions. Let this be a motto as you read through these: living a liberated life is more challenging than living under the Moses Era.

First, we are no longer slaves. This passage opens with the idea of inheritance (4:1) with words connected to the last line of chapter three. Faith connected both Judean and gentile believers to Abraham's promise and made them heirs of that promise. Paul now decides to develop the idea of heir and inheritance as he had developed the idea of promise and covenant.

There's a catch. Heir doesn't change a person's status until they receive the inheritance. In Galatians 4:1–6, Paul adds some new words to the three columns in the timeline on page 105.

Promise Era: promise of inheritance of the estate

Moses Era: no better than slaves, under guardians and trustees, "underage," enslaved to the "elemental spiritual forces of the world"

Christ Era: arrival of the time set, Son is born of Mary, to redeem those "under the law," so believers can be adopted into God's family, Spirit in our hearts, now say "Abba, Father," no longer a slave but God's child

⇨ Heir!

We can't forget what he's doing in this letter. The shift from the Moses Era to the Christ Era puts the Moses Era in our rearview mirror, and that means "works of the law" are not required for gentile converts to Jesus.

Paul uses a most interesting term that calls for explanation. The NIV has "elemental spiritual forces of the world" in 4:3, and in 4:9 he colors those elemental forces a bit with some adjectives: "weak and miserable forces." Behind these verses is the Greek term *stoicheia*, sometimes used for the "ABCs" of life and other times for basic principles (deSilva), like earth, water, fire, wind, stars, sun, and moon. Thus, these elements focus on the created order or cosmic spiritual forces (principalities and powers). But in Galatians 4 those are not his focus. The ABCs, or the basic elements of life, seems closer to the lens, but as deSilva observes, the elemental forces are not seen positively. Rather, they evoke the spiritual power structures and the ways of the world. Paul goes radical. The law of Moses is one of these ABCs of the world because it, too, cuts up humans into groups and works against the unity that Christ brings in the Spirit (3:28). Shaye Cohen, in the *Jewish Annotated New Testament*, comments aptly. This term describes "polytheistic piety previously observed by the Gentile Christians" now applied to the Moses Era! And, "Paul's implicit equation of the two is striking." The law is "akin to the worship of the Greek gods." Furthermore, these elemental forces are anything that creates powers and structures and systems that are not in line with the gospel.

From all this we are liberated to be God's children, to call God "Father," and to be heirs in the line of Abraham. But such a liberation requires not backing up into the Moses Era.

Second, we are daughters and sons of God now.
Paul shifts from a *legal* heir to *adopted* heir (v. 5) because
humans are not naturally children of God. Gentiles and
Jews, slaves and free, women and men become children of
God and siblings of one another by adoption, the legal process of making someone a family member. It is insensitive
to realities to translate, as the NIV does, with "adoption to
sonship" (4:5). That may be a literal translation, but in light
of Galatians 3:28's expansiveness, we are better off translat-
ing it "adoption into the family" or "being placed into a new
family" so that we become "sons *and daughters*" of God. We
become—wait for it—*siblings of Jesus the Son of God*!

Third, we relate to God as our Father. Calling God
"Father" has become so common we may miss its cutting
edge. The evidence of our adoption is how we talk. We
now call God "Father," which in Aramaic is *Abba.* Israelites
did not typically call God "Father" and did not pray, as
Christians do, with the opening "Our Father" or "Our
heavenly Father." None of the psalms open with "Father."
(But it must be insisted that the Old Testament does at
times refer to God as "Father.") Jesus experienced God as
Father himself. He is the Son to the Father, and so Jesus
emphasized addressing God as "Father." Every one of his
prayers, except the famous "cry of dereliction" (Mark
15:34), begins with "Father." Which is why Jesus taught
the disciples to begin prayer by calling God "Father" (Luke
11:2). He drew them into his own experience of God as
Father. Calling God "Father" brings our relationship to
God into the family, expressing our intimacy with God.
But we can only relate to God as Father *because of the Spirit
in us.* All of this is part of our calling God "Father."

Fourth, we are heirs. Paul's "paragraph" neatly emphasizes one term: "heir." Remember, 3:29 ended with heir,
4:1 begins on the note of heir, and 4:7, the conclusion to
his adoption theme, announces we are heirs. The father in
his will designates property to his children, and that property is his until his death, even if he can dispose of some
of it (Luke 15:11–32). Along with the property comes the
status and authority of ownership. This inheritance is the
covenant redemption originally promised to Abraham and
now given in its fullness in Christ through the Spirit.

Some of us (me!) are tempted to make this abstract
theology. We are also tempted to lack empathy for Paul's
critics and those backing up to Moses. So, let me put it
this way: these believers are being asked to join a brand-
new movement (Christianity) based on an old movement
(Moses and Judaism). They are being asked even more to
live a life based on an invisible Holy Spirit. They are being
asked for a full commitment to an unfamiliar group by
jumping out of a familiar Moses Era into an unfamiliar
Christ Era. Perhaps we could resonate with them by pon-
dering sometime when we changed our mind on something
symbolically significant, like changing denominations, or
one's translation of the Bible, or one's beliefs about race
and systemic injustices. It can take a while to adjust into
new instincts, and I believe that's what the Galatians were
experiencing.

Fifth, we must not back up. Paul's turns to how adoption and liberation work. Now focusing on the gentiles
who are being pushed by Paul's critics into observing the
law of Moses, Paul states the specifics. They have assumed
the observance of the Judean calendar ("special days and

months and seasons") like Passover and Rosh Hashanah and Booths. So Paul urges them not to turn back by asking them two questions in 4:9:

How is it that you are turning back to those weak and miserable forces?
Do you wish to be enslaved by them all over again?

Again, look at the chart on page 105. They have moved from the Moses Era to the Christ Era, but taking on the observance of the law of Moses as the completion of their mature response to salvation is actually moving out of the Christ Era back into the Moses Era. They have experienced redemption in Christ—"known by God" (4:9)—but they are putting it all into jeopardy by abandoning the Spirit's power and life in Christ, thinking the way forward is going backward!

Our actions express where we are in relation to God.

If we call God "Abba, Father,"
and if we walk in the Spirit,
and if we fellowship at table with all in Christ,
we embody the Christ Era.

But,

if claiming to be in Christ we follow the Jewish calendar
and require circumcision
and observe food laws,
we have turned from the Christ Era back to the Moses Era.

Paul wonders aloud if he has not wasted his time with the Galatians (4:11).

QUESTIONS FOR REFLECTION AND APPLICATION

1. What are some ways living a liberated life can be harder than living a law life?

2. How does it affect your understanding of these passages to read the added/changed words of daughters and siblings and family instead of just sons and sonship?

3. What are the five dimensions of the liberated life?

4. Of those five dimensions, which means the most to you, and why?

5. Have you ever had an experience of moving into a "quiet" life and realizing you had been used to living with "buzz"? What was that like?

FOR FURTHER READING

Shaye J. D. Cohen, "Galatians," in the *Jewish Annotated New Testament* (Oxford: Oxford University Press, 2017), quoting from 332, 339.

David deSilva, Galatians, New International Commentary on the New Testament (Grand Rapids: Wm. B. Eerdmans, 2018), 348–353.

Krister Stendahl, *Paul among the Jews and Gentiles and Other Essays* (Philadelphia: Fortress, 1976), 78–96.

MOTHERING
LIBERATION

Galatians 4:12–20

¹² *I plead with you, brothers and sisters, become like me, for I became like you. You did me no wrong.* ¹³ *As you know, it was because of an illness that I first preached the gospel to you,* ¹⁴ *and even though my illness was a trial to you, you did not treat me with contempt or scorn. Instead, you welcomed me as if I were an angel of God, as if I were Christ Jesus himself.* ¹⁵ *Where, then, is your blessing of me now? I can testify that, if you could have done so, you would have torn out your eyes and given them to me.* ¹⁶ *Have I now become your enemy by telling you the truth?*

¹⁷ *Those people are zealous to win you over, but for no good. What they want is to alienate you from us, so that you may have zeal for them.* ¹⁸ *It is fine to be zealous, provided the purpose is good, and to be so always, not just when I am with you.* ¹⁹ *My dear children, for whom I am again in the pains of childbirth until Christ is formed in you,* ²⁰ *how I wish I could be with you now and change my tone, because I am perplexed about you!*

There are times to go personal, to express personal disappointment, to express your feelings and explain your emotions. We can tie this passage to the last verse of the previous passage. At Galatians 4:11, Paul expressed fear ("I fear for you") and a feeling of exasperation ("that somehow I have wasted my efforts on you"). How many parents have wanted to say this? How many mentors and leaders and pastors and teachers have muttered these words to themselves or those closest to them? I love this about Paul: his feelings are in his face and words.

We might recall how he opened this letter with an "I am astonished" (1:6). Same feelings of fear and exasperation. But instead of turning on the Galatians, he backs up and ponders how to start all over again. Out of his emotionally cleared mind we find three lessons for teaching others how to live the liberated life, but as N. T. Wright says it, the words of this passage are "a series of rapid-fire commands, comments, questions, and polemical sideswipes" (280).

USE YOUR EXAMPLE

Paul calls attention to his own life to urge the Galatians not to walk back from the Christ Era. We can't be sure what he means when he says, "Become like me, for I became like you" (4:12), but most agree that he's referring to his act of denying exclusive privilege for Judean believers when both he and Peter realized redemption was by faith in Christ and not by the "works of the law" (2:15–21). A few years after writing Galatians, Paul says, "To those not having the law I became like one not having the law (though I am not free from God's law but am under Christ's law), so as to win those not having the law" (1 Cor. 9:21). When he says he became like them he means he has set aside observance of the law of Moses as a way of life in order to reach those—like the Galatians—who are non-observant. In telling his story, he says: I (and Peter) do not believe God's way is in the Moses Era any longer so become like us. Acting like Paul is the same as living a life of liberation (Gal. 5:1). They are instruments and vocals of Paul's music for the Galatians.

He turns now to an even more personal and vulnerable part of his story in 4:13–14. He preached the gospel in Galatia, not because it was on his schedule of events but because he was weakened by some illness. You may recall that in another letter Paul talked about the "thorn in my flesh" (2 Cor. 12:7). If we connect these two passages, we may wonder if Paul had a long-term condition. What we do know is that his condition led some to treat him with "contempt or scorn," words that could more graphically be translated as devaluing his status or spit out at his presence. This could suggest his appearance was less than desirable and perhaps some would have been tempted to think he was under some curse of the gods (or the elemental forces). To tell a story of your own physical inabilities or undesirables or even of one's rhetorical weaknesses is to make one vulnerable to others. Some do this to manipulate an audience, but Paul says the Galatians, instead of spitting at his condition, welcomed him as if he were an "angel of God"! No, he goes deeper: "as if I were Christ Jesus himself"! Yikes. In verse 15 he says that had they been able to tear out their eyes for him they would have—and that might be where his weakness and thorn in the flesh were (Dunn).

Paul explains his feelings and tells his story, to be sure, to get them to see where they were is where they need to be again. As they received him then, they should receive him now. He's not telling his story so he can be magnified. He's telling his story so they'll enter the Christ story and magnify Chriot (Barclay).

ASK QUESTIONS

As Paul often does when he comes to what he most wants from the Galatians, he asks a question or two. By the way, he asks at least eleven questions in Galatians, and when the reader of this letter performed it, he or she would have paused after each one, waited, and often would have entertained answers. His two questions here are:

- Where, then, is your blessing of me now?
- Have I now become your enemy by telling you the truth?

Previously he was an angel or even Jesus himself, but now he's just one to be spit on and has become, in effect, their "enemy."

Paul has been pushed to the margin because he has told them the truth. The feelings at work in asking this second question suggest either exaggeration or, more likely, some kind of irony or even sarcasm. He told them the truth and all over again it is that the Moses Era has moved into the Christ Era and "works of the law" are no longer the proper response to God. Rather, the proper response is faith in the power and fruit of the Spirit (5:16–18).

It does no good to sugarcoat this with what is so popular today, a conference on "Two Views of the Christian Life," one side arguing for "Observe the Law" and another contending for "Life in the Spirit." All being dismissed with a sense of civility and accomplishment, with some hard feelings, but not at all where Paul was. One side was wrong and his side was right! There are, of course, times for genuine agreement about disagreements, but there are other times when disagreement is wrong. When it comes to the Moses Era, it's wrong now; it's time to live in the Christ Era.

The truth involves accurate description of one's critics (4:17–18). Paul knows the zeal of a zealot because he was one himself (Acts 8:1; 9:1–2; Gal. 1:23). He knows they are "zealous to win you over," which is the language of the missionary seeking conversions. This reminds of Jesus' own strong words: "Woe to you, teachers of the law and Pharisees, you hypocrites! You travel over land and sea to win a single convert, and when you have succeeded, you make them twice as much a child of hell as you are" (Matt. 23:15). Paul's accurate description means explaining their intention: "what they want is to alienate you from us" (Gal. 4:17), that is, they are tribalistic, and he adds "so that you may have zeal for them," which echoes those words of Jesus. The critics of Paul are sectarian theologians out to convert people from the Christ Era to the Moses Era, all the while thinking they are improving the Pauline mission! No wonder Paul goes sarcastic. (He's not against zeal or passion or ambition for the gospel, but they better be "good." So Galatians 4:18.)

SHOW YOUR HEART

I fainted in the delivery room of our first child, Laura. For our second, Lukas, I was banned to the waiting room. I speak about labor from a lack of experience. I was a failed father as one who could not handle what it means to be a mother! Not Paul. A few times he fashions himself into a mother (Gaventa), but only moms have mom genes (Tucker). It's worth reading each verse carefully.

He can be a **nursing** mother:

Just as a nursing mother cares for her children, so we cared for you (1 Thess. 2:7–8).

He can be a **birthing** mother:

My dear children, for whom I am again in the pains of childbirth until Christ is formed in you (Gal. 4:19).

He can be **cosmic mother participating in God's birthing mission**:

We know that the whole creation has been groaning as in the pains of childbirth right up to the present time. Not only so, but we ourselves, who have the firstfruits of the Spirit, groan inwardly as we wait eagerly for our adoption to sonship, the redemption of our bodies (Rom. 8:22–23).

This is not manly for Paul to say. This coaxes the charges of being un-Roman, un-Greek, and un-Judean for a man to describe himself as a mother. But those descriptions alone convey the emotions of Paul, what is in his heart for the Galatians.

Paul's famous mission to the gentiles and the consternations it created among his congregations was propelled by a mother's heart. The mother-heart of Paul wanted one thing: for the Galatians to live in the Christ Era and cease the desire to back into the Moses Era. All he wants for his churches is Christoformity—"until Christ is formed in you" (Gal. 4:19).

He finishes with more exasperation as he says he'd like to be there, eating with them and looking into their eyes and hearing them say what they want and looking into their faces and knowing their hearts.

Why? "I am perplexed about you!" Now that's a mother.

QUESTIONS FOR REFLECTION AND APPLICATION

1. What do you think about the image of Paul as a mother? Is that something you had considered before? How does it impact your view of him?

2. What do you think Paul's illness and thorn in the flesh might have been?

3. What are Paul's three lessons for turning around relationships with "children" (the spiritual or the physical kind)?

4. Which of the three lessons do you find to be the hardest to implement as a parent/teacher/leader/mentor?

5. Can you think of a time you have had a "genuine disagreement about agreement" with another Christian—a time when you agreed to disagree over something that wasn't vital to the faith? How does that compare with times you have thought another Christian was genuinely wrong and you were right?

FOR FURTHER READING

John Barclay, "Paul's Story: Theology as Testimony,"
in Bruce Longenecker, ed., *Narrative Dynamics in
Paul: A Critical Assessment* (Louisville: Westminster
John Knox, 2002), 133-156.

James D. G. Dunn, *The Theology of Letter to the
Galatians*, New Testament Theology (Cambridge:
Cambridge University Press, 1993), 236 (on eyes).

Beverly Gaventa, *Our Mother Saint Paul* (Louisville:
Westminster John Knox, 2007).

Abigail Tucker, *Mom Genes: Inside the New Science of
Our Ancient Maternal Instinct* (New York: Gallery,
2021).

READING THE SCRIPTURES AS LIBERATION

Galatians 4:21–31[1]

21 Tell me, you who want to be under the law, are you not aware of what the law says? 22 For it is written that Abraham had two sons, one by the slave woman and the other by the free [liberate] woman. 23 His son by the slave woman was born according to the flesh, but his son by the free [liberate] woman was born as the result of a divine promise.

24 These things are being taken figuratively: The women represent two covenants. One covenant is from Mount Sinai and bears children who are to be slaves: This is Hagar. 25 Now Hagar stands for Mount Sinai in Arabia and corresponds to the present city of Jerusalem, because she is in slavery with her children. 26 But the Jerusalem that is above is free [liberate], and she is our mother. 27 For it is written:

---

1. I have purposely edited the NIV to use the word "liberate" rather than "free" so as to keep the translation consistent with the overarching theme of Galatians.

"Be glad, barren woman,
 you who never bore a child;
shout for joy and cry aloud,
 you who were never in labor;
because more are the children of the desolate woman
than of her who has a husband."

[28] *Now you, brothers and sisters, like Isaac, are children of promise.* [29] *At that time the son born according to the flesh persecuted the son born by the power of the Spirit. It is the same now.* [30] *But what does Scripture say? "Get rid of the slave woman and her son, for the slave woman's son will never share in the inheritance with the free [liberate] woman's son."* [31] *Therefore, brothers and sisters, we are not children of the slave woman, but of the free [liberate] woman.*

We already watched Paul find six different Scriptures, thread them like beads on a string, press them tightly together, and create a bracelet-like design. That's Galatians 3:6–14. He now shows the versatility of his approach to Scripture with allegory. A method as Judean as kosher food laws and a method commonly observed in the history of the church. The critics of Paul at Galatia, upon hearing this passage read aloud, may have done some harumphing, but they would also have admired Paul's Bible skills.

Jesus told a parable about wheat and weeds, which can look almost identical in the growing process. A farmer sowed seeds of wheat by day, the enemy sowed weeds by night, the plants grew up together, some wondered if they ought to pluck the weeds, the farmer said wait until harvest time, and we'll keep the wheat and burn the weeds. Then he "allegorized" the elements of the story: the farmer is Jesus, the field is the world, the wheat the people of God, the sower of weeds is the devil, the weeds the enemies of God, the harvesters are the angels, and the harvest is the final judgment, when God will do the judging—the people of God will be saved, the enemies will be tossed into the blazing furnace. All told in Matthew 13:24–30, 36–43. When someone assigns separable identities and meanings to the various elements of a story, one is allegorizing a story. Philo, a Jewish theologian-philosopher in Alexandria at the time of Jesus, does this often in his writings.

David deSilva calls what Paul does in this passage above a "virtuoso interpretation," while James D. G. Dunn speaks here of Paul, in a "more relaxed mood" showing his "skills as an exegete and the elegance with which he can document his case from scripture." I grew up hearing preachers like Charles Spurgeon and reading devotional books like John Bunyan's *Pilgrim's Progress* that allegorized both characters and events in the Bible. To allegorize, as Paul does in Galatians 4:21–31, requires two features: a text that can be used and a theology that sees itself in the characters and events in that text. Let this be said. If the theology at work is sound, the results are sound; if the theology is corrupted, the results are too. Paul's allegory makes use of his sound theology. The Moses Era and the Christ Era can be described as slavery and liberation.

If you read all of Paul's letters from Romans to Philemon, you will find allegory only twice, a shorter example in 1 Corinthians 9:9–10 and this longer example in Galatians 4. An expert on how Jews read the Bible, Richard Longenecker has suggested something I find reasonable. Paul flips on its head what his critics had been doing with this passage. In fact, Longenecker contends Paul flips his critics' script in four ways. It's guesswork, in part, but it's reasonable. (1) Paul pushes faith in Genesis 15:6 (by faith) when his opponents push circumcision (17:4–14), (2) Paul pushes for Abraham while his critics push for Moses, (3) Paul pushes for a gentile blessing in the promise while they push for a view of the "seed" that is the election of Israel, and (4) his critics said Paul's converts, still not committed fully to the law, were in the line of Ishmael, but their own converts, now fully embracing the law, are in the line of Isaac. Yes, admittedly, one has to infer these observations, but it makes good sense of the emotional, polemical nature of this letter. His critics at times have gotten under his skin with how they read the Bible, so he gives them another reading.

We return to the three periods of God's redemptive work. Paul uses the same periods in this allegory, but this time he brings onto the stage (as it were) Sarah and Hagar, Isaac and Ishmael, as well as Jerusalem Above and Mount Sinai (present Jerusalem). Paul collapses the Promise Era with the Christ Era, so what he says of Abraham and Sarah and Isaac is being said of the Christ Era. Just in case you are wondering, that's what allegory does!

The explanations of each column are close at hand. Paul's theology is one of liberation in the Christ Era and slavery in the Moses Era. Paul's gospel of liberation is seen, if one has an eye to see it, in the stories about Hagar and

Sarah and Isaac and Ishmael. There is nothing new in this Story other than the characters. Perhaps there is one new element: the theme of persecuted/persecutors was not part of the original chart. The big story remains the same: the move from the Moses Era to the Christ Era was a move from slavery to liberation. "Works of the law" enslaves; life in Christ in the power of the Spirit frees the believer.

THREE ERAS IN THE STORY OF ISRAEL

LAW	PROMISE/CHRIST
	Abraham
Slavery	Liberation
Slave woman	Free woman
Hagar	Sarah
Ishmael	Isaac
Flesh son	Promise son
Covenant #1	Covenant #2
Mount Sinai (present Jerusalem)	Jerusalem above
Enslaved children	Liberated children
Persecutors	Persecuted
Born of the flesh	Born of the Spirit
No inheritance	Inheritance

Paul's critics sometimes got under his skin, but what he does in this passage surely got under theirs. To suggest they—fully invested observers of Moses, Bible-on-their-side types—are not successors of Isaac but Ishmael punches their gut, to say they are Hagar's and not Sarah's children kicks their shins, and to say they have no Abrahamic inheritance, well, that chases them out of the land.

> Wouldn't you just love to hear the response of Paul's critics?
> Do you think they caved in or dug in their heels?

What to do? Paul gives the mic to Sarah. In Genesis 21, Sarah observes Ishmael mocking Isaac when Isaac is given a great feast to celebrate the heir. So Sarah tells Abraham to "get rid of that slave woman and her son!" Those words become Paul's words to the gentile believers in Galatia. They, too, are to banish the views and proponents of the return to the Moses Era.

Recall how Paul opened this passage. With one of his well-timed but pointed questions: "Tell me, you who want to be under the law, are you not aware of what the law says?" (4:21). Paul has now given his allegorical reading of the law, a reading his critics both had to respect but surely didn't like. God invaded the life of Paul on the Road to Damascus, shattered his entire worldview based on observance of the law of Moses, and then revealed to him a shockingly fresh way to read the Bible. "Start with Abraham's promise, Paul, and read the whole Bible over again!" However Paul learned it, that's his "hermeneutic" for Bible reading. His critics thought Moses updated

GALATIANS

Abraham and Paul said, "No, Moses had a limited purpose for a limited time. That time is over, and the time now is the fulfillment of the Abrahamic promise in Jesus Christ."

Liberation, or freedom, remains the key word in this letter, and it will come to fruition at the top of the next chapter. What Paul wants is for the Galatians to continue in the experience of redemptive liberation—what we gain in the death of Christ for our sins and what the Spirit empowers us to become.

Easy to say, hard to live out. Freedom is far more of a challenging life than law.

QUESTIONS FOR REFLECTION AND APPLICATION

1. What two things does one need in order to create a scriptural allegory?

2. How does Paul depict the Moses Era and the Christ Era in his allegory?

3. Explain the role or meaning of each of the characters in Paul's allegory here.

4. How do you think Paul's critics received and responded to the new reading of Genesis he gave them?

5. If you were going to create a fresh allegory to explain Paul's ideas in Galatians, what would you say?

FOR FURTHER READING

David deSilva, Galatians, New International Commentary on the New Testament (Grand Rapids: Wm. B. Eerdmans, 2018), 391.

James D. G. Dunn, *The Theology of the Letter to the Galatians,* New Testament Theology (Cambridge: Cambridge University Press, 1993), 243.

Richard Longenecker, *Biblical Exegesis in the Apostolic Period,* 2nd ed. (Grand Rapids: Wm. B. Eerdmans, 1999), 109–113.

LIBERATED FOR LIBERATION

Galatians 5:1–12

[1] *It is for freedom [or liberation] that Christ has set us free [or, liberated us]. Stand firm, then, and do not let yourselves be burdened again by a yoke of slavery.*

[2] *Mark my words! I, Paul, tell you that if you let yourselves be circumcised, Christ will be of no value to you at all.* [3] *Again I declare to every man who lets himself be circumcised that he is obligated to obey the whole law.* [4] *You who are trying to be justified by the law have been alienated from Christ; you have fallen away from grace.* [5] *For through the Spirit we eagerly await by faith the righteousness for which we hope.* [6] *For in Christ Jesus neither circumcision nor uncircumcision has any value. The only thing that counts is faith expressing itself through love.*

[7] *You were running a good race. Who cut in on you to keep you from obeying the truth?* [8] *That kind of persuasion does not come from the one who calls you.* [9] *"A little yeast works through the whole batch of dough."* [10] *I am confident in the Lord that you will take no other view. The one who is throwing you into confusion, whoever that may be, will*

have to pay the penalty. [11] Brothers and sisters, if I am still preaching circumcision, why am I still being persecuted? In that case the offense of the cross has been abolished. [12] As for those agitators, I wish they would go the whole way and emasculate themselves!

When I asked Becky Castle Miller, who writes the questions in our *Everyday Bible Studies*, about the terms "liberation" and "freedom," she made an insightful observation: the terms have been politicized, and she hates that. The political right likes "freedom," and the political left likes "liberation." I have chosen to alternate terms in these guides, but I favor liberation. Let's admit Becky's right about the political spectrum's use of the terms, and let's also move on to Paul's uses—*eleuthero* and *eleutheria*.

Before we press into these great, great words, I want you to consider the problem Paul's critics were seeing.

New converts: "How should we live?"
Some: "Follow the law of Moses."
Paul: "Do what the Spirit tells you to do!"

If you are a disciple maker, which is easiest to choose? Paul's critics had the longer end of this stick. So Paul had an uphill battle to convince the gentiles and his critics that in the Christ Era we don't return to Moses. We instead listen for the Spirit's guidance. (I don't believe many Christians actually believe this. It's frightening for parents to tell their teens to learn to listen to the Spirit when "Don't take drugs!" is so much clearer.)

What does liberation or freedom mean?

THE SIX SENSES OF OUR
LIBERATION IN CHRIST

One of the truly great commentators on Galatians, Hans Dieter Betz, once said freedom "is the basic concept underlying Paul's argument throughout the letter." So I begin with a **first** observation: Liberation is *the central implication of the Christian life*. This entire letter is shaped toward 5:1, which reads (in an overly literal translation), "For liberation . . . us . . . Christ liberated." Four words, the first and last being liberation-words.

Second, we are *free in relation to God*. Because of Christ's death on the cross, his becoming a curse to take on our curse, the believer is liberated from the curse (3:10–14) and from sin (Rom. 6:18, 20, 22; 8:2) and we are adopted in God's family (Gal. 4:5). I write this during the COVID-19 pandemic. Many of us experienced a liberation back into society with greater safety through a second vaccination dose. I know both Kris and I felt this. (First argh. And we also feel "here we go again" with the rise of the Delta variant. Second argh.)

Third, *we are liberated by the power of the Spirit*. I love 2 Corinthians 3:17, which expresses the heart of Galatians: "Now the Lord is the Spirit, and where the Spirit of the Lord is, there is freedom." Our second and third observations come to full expression in Romans 8:2: "because through Christ Jesus the law of the Spirit who gives life has set you free from the law of sin and death." Liberation is a work of God for us and in us. Christian liberation does not turn us free to do whatever we want but liberates us to do what God designed for us to want. The idea that freedom is a liberation into what is good was something known in the world of Paul. For instance, Epictetus said "there is no bad man who lives as he wills, and accordingly no bad man is free" (*Discourses* 4.1.3). It was the Boomer generation, let's be honest, my generation, that formed the view that liberation meant being who you wanted to be and doing what you wanted to do, regardless of social constraints and moral categories. Not so with Paul. Spirit-liberation is for a Spirit-life.

Fourth, *we are free from the law of Moses in the Christ Era*. Paul shapes his understanding of liberation on the rocky surface of polemics. His critics may well think Paul is a loosey-goosey liberal, but Paul thinks they are failing to read the Bible right. In Galatians 2:4 Paul said it: "some false believers" had sneaked into the group "to spy on the freedom we have in Christ Jesus" but their goal was more than discovery. They wanted to "make us slaves," which by now is clear. Paul knew they wanted to move the gentile believers back into the Moses Era with circumcision, food laws, and Sabbath practices. Paul says, "Nope, we are liberated from the Moses Era. Christ has come. Moses did his job. We are living in a new world."

Fifth, *we are liberated to become what God designed us to be*. We enter now into the personal and even existential sense of liberation. We have been set free, not to do what we want but to do what God designed us to want and to be. We have been liberated to become like Christ. I return to the verse after that beautiful verse in 2 Corinthians, this time to verse 18. Read it slowly:

And we all, who with unveiled faces contemplate the Lord's glory, are being transformed into his image with ever-increasing glory, which comes from the Lord, who is the Spirit.

As we gaze into the face of our Lord, we are being transformed by God into the image of Christ. "Look at Jesus!" is the call for redemption and "Look at Jesus!" is also a call for transformation. We are set free from sin and the curse and death and the law so we can be liberated into a life of growing to be like Christ, of what can be called "Christoformity." Our liberation, paradoxically, becomes slavery to Christ (1 Cor. 7:22), to God (Rom. 6:22), and to righteousness (6:18).

Sixth, *we are liberated into a new, inclusive community.* Freedom and Galatians 3:28 hold hands. We have been liberated from our entitlements and privileges and statuses: race, ethnicity, social status, economic status, and gender— all these categories that restrict are now transcended in Christ. We are to embody a new kind of community in a world that enforces and systematizes those categories. We become dissidents against those restrictions by breaking down the walls that divide.

Therefore, as Paul says it, "Stand firm" in this liberated life and don't return to the Moses Era (5:1).

CONSIDER THE CONSEQUENCES

Those who choose to surrender their liberation in Christ to return to the Moses Era need to realize what that return means (5:2–4). Some readers will get tripped up on whether or not Paul thinks someone can lose their salvation, and his words have been understood that way by some. His words, while they seem to indicate that, need to be taken as very strong warnings. Those who abandon the Christ Era for the Moses Era are, in effect, abandoning Christ. This is the language of what Christians have classically called apostasy. Paul says the act of a gentile believer undergoing the blade embodies rejection of the sufficiency of Christ's redemptive power. "Christ will be of no value to you" (5:2). To undergo the rite of circumcision embodies completing Jesus with Moses, and also requires a person to come under the dictates of Moses. Moses, as we have seen, brings a curse and death and cannot lead to life and the inheritance. That rite embodies that one thinks one is made right—"justified"— "by the law," but Paul declares such persons "have been alienated from Christ" (the Christ Era) and "have fallen away from grace," which comes in Christ alone (5:4).

There's only one Christian word for this: apostasy. There's only one consequence: final condemnation. This is what Paul wants the gentile believers to perceive about what they are tempted to do. The consequences can't be any more serious.

Actions often symbolize allegiances. Some place a political party slogan on their bumper to tell the world of their allegiance; some write up an affirmation of a theologian or a pastor on their social media to announce to others their team. Discerning eyes perceive allegiances in actions, but sometimes the discernments can be mistaken and exaggerated. In Paul's world, to begin practicing Sabbath, to eat only kosher food, or to undergo circumcision was an act that declared allegiance to the Moses Era. The gospel has no tolerance for additions to Christ.

WHAT MATTERS NOW

What matters now is not "works of the law" like circumcision but "faith expressing itself through love" (5:5–6). What matters in the Christ Era is living "through the Spirit" as we long for the completion of being made right. That's right, Paul thinks like Jesus and the other apostles. The kingdom and redemption have been inaugurated, but they are not completed until the fullness of the kingdom arrives (Ladd). Final redemption completes the inauguration of redemption we know now. Paul clearly says here that "righteousness" or "being made right" is not complete until the kingdom of God, which means we are both "right" now but "not totally right until then."

The proper response to God in the Christ Era is not the Moses' Era circumcision. What matters now is "faith expressing itself in love." Faith here is both initial trust and ongoing trust, so it combines faith and faithfulness, what Matthew Bates calls "allegiance." Love is the rugged affective commitment to be with God and others and to be "for" God and others as we grow in Christoformity with others.

Though this theme of centralizing love began with Jesus, Paul is as radical as Jesus is. The heart of the law of Moses is love and the various laws are to be understood as instances of loving others. From the law itself, because of what Jesus said in Mark 12:28–34, Paul rereads the whole law as the law of love. Think about this again. His critics read the whole of the Bible through the law of Moses, and Paul said, "No, we read it through the promise to Abraham." As they taught a love for the law, Jesus and Paul taught the law of love.

PAUL'S CUTTING REMARKS

Paul's critics are still irritating him as he goes back and forth from teaching the gospel of liberation in the Christ Era to his critics' message about returning to the Moses Era. Galatians 5:7–12 are some of his sharpest words, even punning on circumcision. He observes they started well, which reminds us again of 3:1–5, but someone has "cut in on them" and he ends with his exasperated, sarcastic wish that they'd just "emasculate themselves," which simply draws us all into realizing he's telling them just to "cut it off." Strong words. Runners ran from one end of a stadium to another, and they turned back toward the finishing line at a stake, which permitted a cagey runner to cut in front of another just before the stake to slow the opponent down or to force him to the outside.

The second expression, "emasculate themselves," evokes the shameful ancient practice of becoming a eunuch. The careful reader realizes Paul considers gentiles who undergo circumcision as no different than eunuchs.

Someone has cut them off by requiring a cutting rite. That someone is not "the one who calls you" (5:8). Paul wants the gentile believers to comprehend that one little act, like requiring kosher food or Sabbath or circumcision, can't be brushed aside, like what time you prefer for a Sunday service, as one's personal preference that may be seen differently by others. Just a little bit of leaven works its way through the whole lump. These acts contaminate the gospel and ruin it.

Back and forth he goes. A rhetorical strategy from time eternal has been to express confidence in your audience at making the right decision. Parents have tried this one endlessly, at least until the child catches on. But Paul interrupts his strong words in this passage just to say that he's confident they will do the right thing (5:10), only to return right back to his irritation about the critics. Verse 11 surprises: "If I am *still* preaching circumcision" suggests he did at one time. But, we ask, when? (1) Is this perhaps a jab by his critics that asking Timothy to be circumcised, as we read in Acts 16:1–3, shows Paul really does think circumcision is required for gentile converts? (2) Or did his critics claim that, had Paul stayed longer he would have led them all to embrace the law of Moses? (3) Or does this refer to his pre-conversion message, as we can read in Acts 9:1–3? It's hard to know, but it's a fun piece of the puzzle to fit in. Since Paul claims present persecution, which he aligns with being in the Christ Era in Galatians 4:29, we ought to see this "still preaching circumcision" to be something after his conversion—and so the first or second options seem best.

Paul got lost in his irritation, but we know where he is. Gentile believers have moved from the Moses Era to the Christ Era so they are liberated from the works of the law. They now live in the Spirit, which is his next topic (5:13–26), and that's all they need.

They have been set free, not so they can return to slavery, but so they can nurture a life of freedom in the power of the Spirit as they seek to be more like Christ.

QUESTIONS FOR REFLECTION AND APPLICATION

1. Do you agree or disagree that the central implication of the Christian life is liberation? Why?

2. As a disciple maker, parent, mentor, or teacher, what challenges do you find in walking with your students as they discern what the Spirit is saying to them? Do you prefer to give them clear rules to follow?

3. Of Paul's six senses of liberation in Christ, which most stands out to you, and why?

4. Do you prefer the word "freedom" or the word "liberation"? What connotation does each have for you?

5. What do you think about the idea of faith as allegiance? If "actions often symbolize allegiances," what do your actions say about your allegiances?

FOR FURTHER READING

Matthew W. Bates, *Gospel Allegiance* (Grand Rapids: Brazos, 2019).

Hans Dieter Betz, *Galatians: A Commentary on Paul's Letter to the Churches in Galatia* (Philadelphia: Fortress Press, 1979), 255.

George Eldon Ladd, *A Theology of the New Testament*, rev. ed. (Grand Rapids: Wm. B. Eerdmans, 1993).

Some of this is based on Scot McKnight, *Galatians*, NIV Life Application Commentary, 16th ed. (Grand Rapids: Zondervan Academic, 1995), 243–247.

EXPRESSIONS
OF LIBERATION

Galatians 5:13–26

[13] *You, my brothers and sisters, were called to be free. But do not use your freedom to indulge the flesh; rather, serve one another humbly in love.* [14] *For the entire law is fulfilled in keeping this one command: "Love your neighbor as yourself."* [15] *If you bite and devour each other, watch out or you will be destroyed by each other.*

[16] *So I say, walk by the Spirit, and you will not gratify the desires of the flesh.* [17] *For the flesh desires what is contrary to the Spirit, and the Spirit what is contrary to the flesh. They are in conflict with each other, so that you are not to do whatever you want.* [18] *But if you are led by the Spirit, you are not under the law.*

[19] *The acts of the flesh are obvious: sexual immorality, impurity and debauchery;* [20] *idolatry and witchcraft; hatred, discord, jealousy, fits of rage, selfish ambition, dissensions, factions* [21] *and envy; drunkenness, orgies, and the like. I warn you, as I did before, that those who live like this will not inherit the kingdom of God.*

[22] *But the fruit of the Spirit is love, joy, peace,*

forbearance, kindness, goodness, faithfulness, ²³ gentleness
and self-control. Against such things there is no law.
²⁴ Those who belong to Christ Jesus have crucified the flesh
with its passions and desires. ²⁵ Since we live by the Spirit,
let us keep in step with the Spirit. ²⁶ Let us not become
conceited, provoking and envying each other.

You have perhaps been in circles that have some strong theories of how to progress as a Christian: speak in tongues, practice solitude, read some Richard Foster and then some Dallas Willard, listen more to Christian music, keep a daily prayer and reflection journal, one psalm and one chapter of Proverbs per day, 30 minutes of daily Bible reading, join a small group Bible study, and on and on the additions pile up into an endless cycle of frustration. Yes, each of these can be helpful just as knowing the law of Moses could be helpful. But where are we centered? In what we do, in our practices, or in the power of God's grace unleashed by the Spirit in us?

Let's think about all the Christian life as a life of expressions. In this passage Paul thinks of two expressions: expressions of the flesh and expressions of the Spirit. We get hung up here on the list and forget the list is a series of expressions of the Spirit, what Paul calls "fruit" (5:22–23). If you were to ask Paul two months after he wrote this letter what life in the Spirit looked like he might have had a few other words than we find here. He might have said to the Galatians: "Don't obsess over these terms, let the Spirit guide you, and you will look like these fruit *and even more!*" Beginning with the number one expression.

Before we dip into expressions of flesh and expressions

218

of Spirit, I have a question. What behaviors do you think are "flesh," and what behaviors would you assign to "Spirit"? One can think about this in the home, in the neighborhood, in one's church, and at one's workplace. Today one has to think of social media interactions, which often turn to snark and disputations and name-calling, and the next thing you know a person is outraged about something not all that important. And feeling quite good about themselves! Two authors recently devoted a whole book to describing "grandstanding" as the attempt by each of us to get others to think of us as morally respectable, and we attempt to do this by some kind of display of our virtue (Tosi and Warmke). Grandstanding is an expression of the "flesh."

THE NUMBER ONE EXPRESSION

The first expression, or fruit, of the Spirit in 5:22 is "love," but before he gets there, knowing the centrality of love, Paul reiterates what Jesus had taught his followers in the Jesus Creed (Mark 12:28–34). As Jesus quoted Leviticus 19:18, so does Paul, and we need to pause to catch our breath after hearing Paul. "The entire law" means all 613 commands and prohibitions, which means Paul's "fulfilled" claims all 613 arrive at their full design in one simple command: "love your neighbor as yourself" (Gal. 5:14). Paul grew up in Pharisaic Judaism. His teacher was Gamaliel. He was theologically educated in Jerusalem. He bumped elbows with the best—you could say he got a first-century Ivy League degree. He learned to parse and explain and observe the minutest of commands, the kind Jesus gets irritated with in Matthew 23. But when gentile converts to Jesus want to know how to live, Paul does not require a three-year degree in law and rabbinics. He goes straight to Jesus: love others as you love yourself. This is what it means to live in the Spirit. The premier expression of the Spirit is love, and the Spirit-prompted person is one who loves God and loves others. Spirit-ual formation is formation into love. (Read that last sentence a couple more times and write it at the top of the page.)

Problem: in Galatia the believers are at one another's throats, denouncing and damning and destroying (5:15, 26). This is all about the critics pressing gentile believers to observe the law and others, like Paul, fighting back for the freedom of the Spirit. All one has to do is reread Galatians 2:11–14. At the table, they devoured one another, and he warns them that division does more than divide—it destroys.

EITHER-OR

The Spirit and the flesh are polar opposites. Like patriarchy and matriarchy, good and evil, communism and capitalism, light and darkness, Cubs and Yankees. Recall that Paul lined up the flesh with the Moses Era and the Spirit with the Christ Era. That's his argument here. Those who walk in the Spirit will not live out the "acts of the flesh" (5:19–21). Both Spirit and flesh want control of a person's life.

The term "flesh" in Paul's writing refers to the unredeemed person, the patterns of sin established in one's previous-to-conversion life, habits that sometimes break through into the life of a believer. It is best to think of flesh like this: we are born into and socialized in a fallen world, we embody some good habits and some bad ones, our habits form our character, and since our habits are not all good, our character gets corrupted. Our corrupted character, like some agent with power in our life, steers us into a deepening of our corrupted actions and character.

The good news is that redemption in Christ cancels our sin, and the Spirit empowers us to overcome the flesh (Dunn). Notice that Paul says the Flesh-as-Agent fights the believer, but this does not mean we are to despair over some war in us that is at an official stalemate. I translate it this way: "these things oppose one another so—whatever you want—these things you don't do." They are not equal forces, but if one surrenders to the flesh, the flesh wins; if one surrenders to the Spirit, the Spirit wins.

EXPRESSIONS OF THE FLESH

Paul uses the term, in my own translation, "manifestations" in 5:19 for the flesh because *flesh versus Spirit* form the oppositions far more than the various expressions of either. Paul knows the fleshy world of the Roman empire for he has traveled from Antioch in Syria to Tarsus and Galatia and will get to Ephesus and Thessalonica and Athens and Greece. Before his conversion, stereotypes of gentile sins were commonly stated in the synagogue, and a good example of how gentiles lived can be found in the sins listed in Romans 1:18–32. Those common criticisms of gentile idolatries and sexual indulgences are transposed here into expressions of the flesh. Gentile unbelievers live in the flesh—that's his worldview. So this list is what's on display when Paul looks out the window at night. His list of flesh expressions contains the noteworthy habits of notorious sinners. His list zooms in on sensual indulgences, idolatry, divisive passions, status-mongering, and more indulgences.

MANIFESTATIONS OF THE SPIRIT

Fruit or produce is the term Paul uses for the expressions of the Spirit. Again, his aim here is Spirit-prompted living more than forming a checklist to see where we stack up. Yes, these are all important Christian virtues, but they are not so much rules that we obey. They are expressions in our relationships with other people when we are walking in the Spirit and are led by the Spirit and live by the Spirit and keep in step with the Spirit (5:16, 18, 25). The Roman world depicted moral improvement through knowledge of what was good and just, by the habit of practicing what was good and just, and these habits produced a good character. Paul's Judean world understood moral improvement as learning the laws of Moses and observing them. Paul would agree with both of these, but only in part.

The part missing was the Spirit. The fullness of the Christ Era brings the grace and power of the Spirit that comes to expression in age-defying transformed living.

The Spirit generates the fruit. Many have tried to organize the fruit of the Spirit, none all that convincing but all of them suggestive. Some see them in relation to God, to others, and to self. Yes, and more. It is safe to see them all as *relational* ethics, but especially our relationship with others. The Christ Era is the era of the church, the family of God, the family of Abraham. The ethic of the Christ Era therefore is an ethic that instructs believers how to get along with people who are different (3:28). We are to love all these different others, and to be at peace with others, to have forbearance with others, to be kind to others, to be good in our relationships (McKnight and Barringer), to be faithful to one another and to God, to be gentle with one another, and to be in control of ourselves. Here's a vital observation about ethics for Paul: *we need others so that we can live as Christians because Christian living is about learning to live like Christ with others.* We are one, so our life is about learning to live as one. Sometimes our focus in the modern world is so much with ourselves—notice he has only one word for our relationship to ourselves—that we forget the primary virtue is "love" and love is a relationship with someone else! A great question for us to evaluate our Christian character is, "How do I relate to others?" These various relational ethics are all the fruit of the Spirit, expressions of the Spirit doing what the Spirit alone can do.

OPEN TO THE SPIRIT

When I was seventeen years old, my plans were to go to a university on a track scholarship as a high jumper or perhaps a decathlete. Don't laugh because it was true. I was decent enough to get scholarship inquiries. In the summer before my senior year, I was at a Christian camp, mostly to horse around and cause problems and have fun with my girlfriend (Kris, now my wife!). On the first night, the

223

main Bible teacher came to our senior high boys' cabin and talked with us. He told us we needed to spend time thinking about being "filled with the Spirit," and the verse he quoted was "And be not drunk with wine, wherein is excess; but be filled with the Spirit" (Ephesians 5:18 KJV). We were all King James in those days. The next morning, before breakfast, I wandered down to the little outdoor chapel, sat down under a big oak tree, and prayed what he asked us to pray. I simply said, "Father, forgive me of my sins and fill me with the Spirit."

It happened.

All I can say is that from that moment I was a different person. I spent that week with Kris and our friends devouring the Bible, praying, attending services, singing, and preparing to become what God called me to be—a teacher of the Bible.

We are to be open to the Spirit the way a glass is open to fresh, cold, living water.

QUESTIONS FOR REFLECTION AND APPLICATION

1. Have you ever felt overwhelmed by expectations for spiritual disciplines required for you to be considered a "good Christian"? Which practices feel like a burden, and which are actually refreshing for you?

2. What is the number one expression of the Spirit? What does it look like lived out?

3. How are the Spirit and the flesh polarized from each other? How does the interplay between them work?

4. Fruit is shown in our relationships with others. Consider the fruit in your relationships. Where do you see fruit of the flesh? Where do you see fruit of the Spirit?

5. The fruit of the Spirit mentioned here in Galatians isn't an exact checklist but an inspirational starting point for your own creativity with the Spirit's unique expression in your life. If you were creating a new pair of lists like Paul's for your culture today, what behaviors would you put in the "flesh" category and what would you assign to "Spirit"?

FOR FURTHER READING

Matthew Croasmun, *The Emergence of Sin: The Cosmic Tyrant in Romans* (New York: Oxford University Press, 2017).

David deSilva, *Transformation: The Heart of Paul's Gospel* (Bellingham, WA: Lexham, 2014).

James D. G. Dunn, *The Theology of Paul the Apostle* (Grand Rapids: Wm. B. Eerdmans, 2006), 62–73.

Scot McKnight, *Open to the Spirit: God in Us, God with Us, God Transforming Us* (Colorado Springs: WaterBrook, 2018).

Scot McKnight, Laura Barringer, *A Church Called Tov* (Carol Stream, IL: Tyndale Momentum, 2020), 83–96.

Justin Tosi, Brandon Warmke, *Grandstanding: The Use and Abuse of Moral Talk* (New York: Oxford, 2020).

FOUR EXAMPLES
OF LIBERATION

Galatians 6:1–10

¹ [1] Brothers and sisters, if someone is caught in a sin, you who live by the Spirit should restore that person gently. But watch yourselves, or you also may be tempted. ² Carry each other's burdens, and in this way you will fulfill the law of Christ. ³ If anyone thinks they are something when they are not, they deceive themselves. ⁴ Each one should test their own actions. Then they can take pride in themselves alone, without comparing themselves to someone else, ⁵ for each one should carry their own load.

⁶ [2] Nevertheless, the one who receives instruction in the word should share all good things with their instructor.

⁷ [3] Do not be deceived: God cannot be mocked. A man reaps what he sows. ⁸ Whoever sows to please their flesh, from the flesh will reap destruction; whoever sows to please the Spirit, from the Spirit will reap eternal life.

⁹ [4] Let us not become weary in doing good, for at the proper time we will reap a harvest if we do not give up. ¹⁰ Therefore, as we have opportunity, let us do good to

all people, especially to those who belong to the family of
*believers. [*Note:* Numbers in brackets have been added.]*

Sometimes wrap-ups summarize all that has been said
and sometimes they take quick looks at uncovered ter-
rain. What Paul gives the Galatians at the end of his letter
is not a new kind of Moses Code. Instead, with one eye on
the tension his mission creates everywhere between Judean
and gentile believers and the other eye on the specifics of
Galatia, Paul gives four examples of what life in Christ looks
like when believers are being transformed by the Spirit of
God. These are not then Paul's Top Four Ethical Principles
but further expressions of Spirit-shaped living in one context at one time. Each one embodies life in the Christ Era.

CARE FOR OTHERS, PROTECTING SELF

Paul catches my attention with an unexpected back and
forth between caring for others while protecting oneself.
He knows that some take on a pastoral task with inad-
equate spiritual formation. He begins in 6:1 with the
instruction to restore those who are "caught in a sin" and
follows that up quickly with "but watch yourselves, or you
also may be tempted." In verse 2 he then turns back to
other-care with "carry each other's burdens" only then to
turn to self-awareness and self-deceit and self-examination
and self-responsibility (6:3–5).

In the last decade, the moral collapse of a number

of well-known evangelical pastors illustrates the need for protection. Protection involves self-awareness, adequate preparation, mentoring by wise leaders, responsible accountability, and most especially character formation. Intelligence and charisma, a seminary degree, exceptional skills on the platform in preaching and telling compelling stories, a burgeoning congregation, and adoring circles of support don't indicate spiritual maturity. Sadly, they activate narcissistic tendencies in pastors and preachers. (All pastors are on the narcissism spectrum. No one who gets up on a stage to speak for God with authority is off the spectrum, DeGroat.)

Age matters. We have a culture that values what is new and what is young and what is physically attractive. The church in the late twentieth century began to place such values on the platforms and behind pulpits, and publishers began to favor such values because they sold books. Youth and maturity rarely walk together, for maturation takes time, longer for some, and so we have increasingly called unprepared persons for one of the most delicate and important callings in society: the preaching pastor. Many of these persons are skilled preachers and so create a persona of maturity when their heart is unformed and their self-awareness untapped. This is not a discourse on preparing or calling pastors, but let this be a final suggestion. Seminarians need to take a solid psychological test in order to become more self-aware, and committees that call pastors need at least one psychologist, fewer lawyers, and fewer CEOs. They also need to rethink whether their candidates should go through a psychological test with someone on the search committee capable of advising the committee on the suitability of the candidate.

Paul's concern, remember, is caring for others. He calls it something that reminds us once again that we are in the Christ Era, for he calls the principle of caring for others the "law of Christ" (6:2). The specific, "carry each other's burdens," embodies that Christ-law. As discussed at Galatians 5:14, the "law of Christ" is the Jesus Creed of loving God and others as oneself (Mark 12:28–34)

GENEROSITY

Out of nowhere Paul turns to sharing one's material resources with one's catechist. Okay, "catechist" is a later church term, but the Greek term Paul uses is *katecheō*, from which we get the term "catechism," and the teacher of a catechism is a catechist. Already by the time Paul writes this letter, at least in Galatia, there are people gifted to be the church's teachers who, in taking time to instruct, are taking time from their work and are thus worthy of material benefits. When Paul says "should share" he refers to material fellowship, the way many of us donate to our church so our pastors and teachers and directors can devote their time to the ministry.

Because there are at times criticisms of paying pastors and preachers and itinerant speakers, I want to record here verses that indicate the early Christian practice of supporting ministers. I ask you to read these Scriptures slowly, noticing that this was a practice already in the days of Jesus' earthly life.

[Acquire/take] no bag for the journey or extra shirt or sandals or a staff, for the worker is worth his keep (Matt. 10:10).

Don't we have the right to eat and drink? . . . Or is it only I and Barnabas who don't have the right to not work for our living? . . . If we sowed spiritual things in you, is it so much to ask to harvest some material things from you? If others have these rights over you, don't we deserve them all the more? In the same way, the Lord has commanded that those who preach the gospel should receive their living from the gospel (1 Cor. 9:4, 6, 11–12, 14 CEB).

Share with the Lord's people who are in need. Practice hospitality. . . . They were pleased to do it, and indeed they owe it to them. For if the Gentiles have shared in the Jews' spiritual blessings, they owe it to the Jews to share with them their material blessings (Rom. 12:13; 15:27).

. . . . they urgently pleaded with us for the privilege of sharing in this service to the Lord's people (2 Cor. 8:4).

. . . because of your partnership in the gospel from the first day until now . . . Moreover, as you Philippians know, in the early days of your acquaintance with the gospel, when I set out from Macedonia, not one church shared with me in the matter of giving and receiving, except you only . . . (Phil. 1:5; 4:15).

There is a perceived "right" to be paid materially for one's spiritual ministry, but there is no obligation on the part of the minister to take the gift. Rather, the church supplies so the minister can carry out her gift with minimal interference. Some, like Paul, chose at times to work day and night at some manual labor job, probably until the church found its sea legs, but there is no demand that the minister do manual labor or be a bi-vocational pastor. Material generosity reciprocates spiritual blessings.

All this to contend that the one who benefits from a teacher of the gospel expresses gratitude in the typical form of first-century reciprocity. The one who receives a gift becomes socially bound to the giver, responds in grateful reciprocal giving, and, contrary to common ancient custom, the giver is not honored with public praise but instead the glory goes to God (Barclay, Downs).

ONE OR THE OTHER

Sharing material resources with one's teacher prompts Paul to articulate a moral axiom: one "reaps what he sows" (6:7). In this short paragraph ([3] in the text above), providing material resources to one's teacher sows "to please the Spirit" and such a sower "will reap eternal life" (6:8). The alternative sows "to please their flesh" and those sowers "will reap destruction" (6:8). The flesh here takes us back to the manifestations of the flesh in 5:19–21, but one might wonder, with his new emphasis on generosity, if the flesh here is self-indulgence with one's resources rather than sharing with one's teacher. Probably so.

Doing Good

"Doing good" in common conversation today means being nice or helping a neighbor, but in the first century the expression takes us into the public sector and to acts of public benevolence, like building bridges, providing grain during a famine, and hosting public events. Caring for the poor was not so common among the Greeks and Romans, though it was inherent in Judaism due to the concern for the poor in the law of Moses. Charitable giving to the poor became an essential virtue for Jesus and his followers and thus passed into the churches Paul established (Longenecker).

Paul calls for Christians to be generous to the poor (2:10), to be generous to all people (6:10), but to be especially generous with fellow believers. This means quite explicitly to have preferential generosity for those in need in our midst without ignoring those in need in our community and nation.

Four patterns of life—caring for others while protecting oneself, generosity, anchoring one's life in the Spirit and not the flesh, and doing good—which is generosity all over again—are expressions of what it means to be liberated by the Spirit in the Christ Era. No law of Moses says it any better. What makes Paul's teachings different is that these four virtues are embodied by the power of the Spirit of God, the gift of the Christ Era.

QUESTIONS FOR REFLECTION AND APPLICATION

1 Paul gives here four examples of what a Spirit-filled life could look like for a community. What are other examples you could add to the list?

2. How does life in the Spirit lead us to a life of generosity?

3. What other suggestions would you add to a list of ideas for helping seminaries and church leadership teams shape truly Christoform pastors?

4. How do the ideas of what constitutes "doing good" differ between the first century and today?

5. What do you think about the obligation of spiritual students to provide for their teachers? Is this something you practice in your life or would like to begin doing?

FOR FURTHER READING

John Barclay, *Paul and the Gift* (Grand Rapids: Wm. B. Eerdmans, 2015).

Chuck DeGroat, *When Narcissism Comes to Church* (Downers Grove, IL: IVP, 2020).

David Downs, *The Offering of the Gentiles* (Grand Rapids: Wm. B. Eerdmans, 2016).

Bruce Longenecker, *Remember the Poor* (Grand Rapids: Wm. B. Eerdmans, 2010).

Scot McKnight, *Pastor Paul* (Grand Rapids: Brazos, 2019), 79-101.

NEW CREATION
LIBERATION

Galatians 6:11–18

[11] *See what large letters I use as I write to you with my own hand!*

[12] *Those who want to impress people by means of the flesh are trying to compel you to be circumcised. The only reason they do this is to avoid being persecuted for the cross of Christ.* [13] *Not even those who are circumcised keep the law, yet they want you to be circumcised that they may boast about your circumcision in the flesh.* [14] *May I never boast except in the cross of our Lord Jesus Christ, through which the world has been crucified to me, and I to the world.* [15] *Neither circumcision nor uncircumcision means anything; what counts is the new creation.* [16] *Peace and mercy to all who follow this rule—to the Israel of God.*

[17] *From now on, let no one cause me trouble, for I bear on my body the marks of Jesus.*

[18] *The grace of our Lord Jesus Christ be with your spirit, brothers and sisters. Amen.*

Paul is like a person fired unjustly who, no matter the conversation, returns to that unjust experience. I can't blame him for returning over and over to the problems roiling in his churches. Galatians is probably the earliest letter of Paul's that we have, and at this juncture in his journey he may well think this letter will solve this problem once and for all. I'd like to tell Paul something that we know now that he didn't know then: "Friend, this tension with Judean believers wanting gentile believers to observe the law of Moses will never go away. So, get ready for the long haul. Some days will be better than others, but the problem is here to stay."

ONE MORE TIME

A motive for his critics' theology and behavior—circumcising gentile believers—now comes to the surface: they are trying to impress people. Who? Almost certainly the men from James, which he also calls the circumcision party. Such persons embody the convictions of the Judean Christians in the home church in Jerusalem, which was the "Vatican" of the earliest churches for one generation (until Jerusalem was destroyed by the Romans in 66–73 AD). He assigns a second motive: "the only reason they do this is to avoid being persecuted for the cross of Christ" (6:12). The scenario now seems clear. The Jerusalem church didn't think Paul's way of discipling gentiles was kosher enough, and they were being pressed by non-believing Judeans in the city of Jerusalem. Those who supported the Pauline mission were under pressure, so some "men from James" are sent out with a pocketknife to get the job done so it would become clear that Paul's missionary work was consistent with the law of Moses.

Paul's response is this letter.

He disagrees. Vehemently. All the way to the end.

The Moses Era comes to its terminus in the Christ Era, and in the Christ Era, the law of Moses is not required. What is required is life in the Spirit that concentrates on love and the fruit of the Spirit.

He not only disagrees. He criticizes all over again with a new wrinkle. "Not even those who are circumcised keep the law" (6:13). There is a stubborn belief in many Christian circles that Paul believed God demanded utter perfection in keeping the law if one wants to be acceptable to God. Since no one does keep the law perfectly, everybody's damned. The only way we can be accepted, then, is by having the perfection of Christ imputed to us by Christ's perfect obedience. So, the argument goes, Paul is saying here that the circumcision party is damned because they're committed to the law as the means of righteousness. Regardless of the clarity and compelling power of this stubborn belief, it is not the world of the Old Testament or of Paul (Sanders). The Bible and Judaism never thought anyone could keep the law perfectly, and that's why the Bible provided sacrificial forgiveness from the very beginning. If one sins, and everyone does, one offers sacrifices—it's called *Yom Kippur*, the Day of Atonement—and one is back in good order. For Paul suddenly to foist on his critics a belief that since they are not perfect their system is wrong is for Paul to use a non-starter, easy-to-refute ("Ever read Leviticus, Paul?") argument.

No, what Paul is doing is reminding the Galatians of the terms in the Moses Era column: law and curse and death. You don't find life and righteousness in that column. Life and righteousness and acceptance and transformation come in the Christ Era through the death and resurrection and ascension of Jesus, who sent the Spirit to transform us.

One More Time, Again

The way to train gentiles is not by returning to the Moses Era. Transformation comes through the cross of Christ, and here Paul returns to Galatians 2:15–21. We all have to die with Christ because it is through dying to the law and to the self that we gain the liberated life. So, Paul wants to boast, not in numbers of gentiles circumcised but in the cross of Christ. The desire to impress others dies on that cross.

Perhaps the most radical statement heard among Paul's critics, and surely within a month it was being reported all over Jerusalem, was this one made by Paul: "Neither circumcision nor uncircumcision *means anything*" (6:15). Again, his critics raise their hands with snark, "What about Genesis 17, Paul?" Paul has now said this twice: circumcision does not matter (5:6 and 6:15). What does matter is "faith expressing itself through love" (5:6) and "new creation" (6:15). If the former emphasized the liberated life of love, this one emphasizes the whole column. The Christ Era is the new creation column (2 Corinthians 5:17).

As we finish this study of Galatians, a few more notes about this last passage. He started off this paragraph by writing himself. Paul did not "write" his letters. He and his coworkers discussed what needed to be said, probably had someone write up a draft or two, and then they hired a professional writer/scribe to put quill to parchment. They made a copy or two of each of his letters, and Paul carried his own letters around with him (Richards). Romans 16:22 tells us Tertius "wrote" out the letter. We don't know who wrote Galatians, but we do know that the reader probably chuckled when she or he got to Galatians 6:11 and noticed the clumsy "large letters" that suddenly appeared. Paul was now writing himself. He does this also in 1 Corinthians 16:21 and Philemon 19. Paul and everyone would have coached the one carrying the letter to Galatia on how to read the letter effectively, and then Paul signed off.

Paul prays a blessing of peace and mercy for all "who follow this rule"—we get our word "canon" from the word "rule" (Greek *kanōn*). The "canon" for Paul embodies three words: New. Creation. Liberation. Those who live this liberated life are the "Israel of God," that is, they are those who live in the Christ Era with Jesus, the Judean Messiah, as their Lord and who live this new creation liberation life. Paul believes the plan of God all along was to bring the promises to Abraham to completion in Christ, and that the Promise Era and the Moses Era were phases of God's work in this world. These two phases are fulfilled in the Christ Era, so the people of God in the Christ Era are now "God's Israel." But this doesn't erase Judean-ness from Judeans or gentile-ness from gentiles. It liberates them to transcend their distinctions in a unity that celebrates both.

His wish is that the troublemakers would go away because he's got on his body the marks of persecution, as

Jesus himself had (6:17). What Paul says in 2 Corinthians 11:23–27 is the best commentary on "the marks of Jesus." I quote:

> Are they servants of Christ? (I am out of my mind to talk like this.) I am more. I have worked much harder, been in prison more frequently, been flogged more severely, and been exposed to death again and again. Five times I received from the Jews the forty lashes minus one. Three times I was beaten with rods, once I was pelted with stones, three times I was shipwrecked, I spent a night and a day in the open sea, I have been constantly on the move. I have been in danger from rivers, in danger from bandits, in danger from my fellow Jews, in danger from Gentiles; in danger in the city, in danger in the country, in danger at sea; and in danger from false believers. I have labored and toiled and have often gone without sleep; I have known hunger and thirst and have often gone without food; I have been cold and naked.

Time would prove that the trouble would remain with him. Everywhere Paul planted a church, Judean believers pressed home the importance of the law of Moses, and out came Paul's chart we formed out of Galatians 3:15–25. Everywhere. All the way to Paul's arrest in Jerusalem in Acts 21 and trials thereafter (Acts 22–26).

It became a custom for Paul to end his letters with a prayer wish that God's blessings and grace would be upon them. It's worth reading slowly.

The grace of our Lord Jesus Christ be with your spirit, brothers and sisters.

Amen.

QUESTIONS FOR REFLECTION AND APPLICATION

1. Summarize the main points of this study in Galatians Try drawing the chart from the opening passage (Galatians 3:15–25) without looking back at it, then check your work.

2. How has this study moved you closer to a life of new creation liberation?

3. How have you felt liberated to be who God created you to be, to live a life of righteousness?

4. What was the most challenging lesson you learned in this study?

5. How have you felt liberated to love others better, to transcend differences and distinctions, to create a unity that celebrates each person?

FOR FURTHER READING

E. Randolph Richards, *Paul and First-Century Letter Writing* (Downers Grove, IL: IVP Academic, 2004).

E. P. Sanders, *Judaism: Practice and Belief* (Minneapolis: Fortress, 2016).